LIVING WITH POETRY

Other Books by Howard L. Schwartz

Women: Biology, Culture and Literature
IPBooks, 2019

Who Would We Be Without Stories: "Human beings need stories as desperately as they need food"
KDP (Kindle Direct Publishing), 2019

In Search of a Wider Audience: Stories, Essays, Poems, and the Psychoanalysis of Dreaming
KDP (Kindle Direct Publishing), 2019

Hide and Seek/Hidden and Found—In Search of a Balanced Life: Psychoanalytic Memoirs, Stories and Essays
IPBooks, 2017

All Aboard
IPBooks, 2017

Living with Poetry
*Finding Something Deep Inside Yourself
That Only Poetry Can Reach*

Howard L. Schwartz, M.D.

International Psychoanalytic Books (IPBooks)
New York • http://www.IPBooks.net

Living with Poetry

Published by IPBooks, Queens, NY
Online at www.IPBooks.net

Copyright © 2020 Howard L. Schwartz, M.D.

All rights reserved. This book may not be reproduced, transmitted, or stored in whole or in any part or by any means, including graphic, electronic, or mechanical without the permission of the author, except in a demonstrated original work of scholarship that might be otherwise accorded a Fair Use exemption for the advancement of the value of reading poetry, with attribution to Howard l. Schwartz, M, D. Brief quotations in critical articles and reviews are permitted without reservation. It is my intention to make this book as available as possible, dedicated to advance the value of poetry in our daily lives.

ISBN: 978-1-949093-84-1

For my children, Ron, Dana, and Leslie,

and my grandchildren

Alexander, Willem, Sabine, Nathaniel, and Eli

ABOUT THE COVER

Steven S. Powers, a painter and Fine Arts dealer, designed the cover as an homage to William Carlos Williams (more later about his *Doctor Stories* and poetry), whose mother had trained as a painter in Paris and passed on her enthusiasm to her son and who also painted in his early years. A painting by him now hangs in the Yale University Beinecke Rare Book and Manuscript Library, and, as late as 1962, he was still remembering in an interview that "I'd like to have been a painter, and it would have given me at least as great a satisfaction as being a poet. "(Wikipedia). For most of his life, Williams wrote art criticism and introductions to exhibitions by his friends. We know that he knew Matisse because of his painting *The Blue Nude*, 1907, by Henri Matisse. The cover design is of an open book, on a table with flowers, waiting to be read, a more abstract invitation to the viewer to read books. Throughout his career, Williams thought of his approach to poetry as a painterly deployment of words, saying explicitly in an interview, "I've attempted to fuse the poetry and painting, to make it the same thing... Design in the poem and design in the picture should make them more or less the same thing."

PERMISSIONS

The poems of the following are gratefully reprinted with the permission of the authors or publishers: Maxine Kumin, Maureen Nelson, Robert Pinsky, Lauren Schwartz, Sabine Bos, Anita Spector, and William Carlos Williams.

Excerpts from various poems from *An American Sunrise: Poems* by Joy Harjo, Copyright © 2019 by Joy Harjo. Used by permission of W. W. Norton & Company, Inc.

"Introduction by Robert Coles" (pp. 12–16, "I bless...") by William Carlos Williams, from *The Doctor Stories*, Copyright © 1984 by Robert Coles, reprinted by permission of New Directions Publishing Corp.

"Born To Run" by Bruce Springsteen; Copyright © 1975 Bruce Springsteen, renewed © 2003 Bruce Springsteen (Global Music Rights). Reprinted by permission. International copyright secured. All rights reserved.

Donika Kelly, "From the Catalogue of Cruelty" from *The Renunciations*. Copyright © 2021 by Donika Kelly. Reprinted with the permission of The Permissions Company, LLC on behalf of Graywolf Press, www.graywolfpress.org.

ACKNOWLEDGMENTS

The works of Robert Pinsky, William Carlos Williams, and Joy Harjo speak to my intentions and aspirations in learning to read, understand, hear and—yes, read out loud—to seek personal meaning in the poetry they write. Without David Denby's *Lit Up*, I would not have appreciated those special teachers who are determined to make readers and informed critics of 10th grade students by getting into the weeds with them, providing them and me with a syllabus to choose from—and the freedom to make independent choices that might make them lifelong readers, and engage me in reading poetry, which in the past "I didn't much favor." Although I have introduced dozens of giants from different traditions and eras in this book, I have read many more of their poems and researched their histories to provide perspective on their work—to get to know the person behind their poems, including the mysterious, hidden intentions— that William Carlos Williams, the doctor, sees as the poem that is in them. My thanks to Matthew Zapruder[1], author of *Why Poetry*, for freeing me up to read poetry... thinking and feeling the poem through for myself without any teachers or books—not quite so as I have already acknowledged Denby's and Zapruder's books—and Zapruder for encouraging me to recognize that at this time in (my) life—as there was in his—"somewhere deep in myself I understood that there was something only poetry could do, a place only a poem could reach, and that I needed that feeling." Zapruder writes, "This book was written not to give all the answers... but to be a starting

---

1 Zapruder, M. (2017). *Why Poetry*. New York: Harper Collins.

point. Reading it should make it more possible for anyone to find the poems that matter to them. Most of all, I hoped that when I was finished with this book, whenever anyone told me they don't know how to read poetry, I could hand them this book and say, I believe just by being alive you already do."

After trying and failing to understand why I undertook this project at age eighty-two, writing this introduction after completing the book and recognizing that much of what I've written reflects feelings about my own mortality, Zapruder hit the nail on the head—deeper in myself there are fears, sadness, and anger that I need to acknowledge. Robert Frost, T.S. Eliot, Maxine Kumin, Mark Twain, William Carlos Williams, Abraham Lincoln, Benjamin Franklin, Joy Harjo, and Robert Pinsky have all helped; but none as much as two women poets, Maureen Nelson and Lauren Schwartz, who have moved me to tears as they shared their pain and with honesty and courage built new lives "with memories in their pockets" (Lauren Schwartz). They have given me written permission to use their poems without any reservations. Maureen introduced me to Haiku and played a friendly game of can-you-top-this with me—back and forth, five-seven-five. I accepted Lauren's gift of forty-three poems, an autobiography in poetry, and incorporated her book, *What Do You Imagine When You Imagine Your Life Without Me?* into my book. No, I haven't forgotten the tears I shed when my granddaughter Sabine, now a poet and essayist about to go off to college, dedicated her first book, as a grammar school child, to grandpa, nor the plethora of poems to follow; at age sixteen she wrote "Inversa"—an almost uncanny empathic appreciation of what awaits all of us, "sinking into the damp bitter air." Now eighteen-years-old, she has given me written permission to use all her poems, including an apt

ACKNOWLEDGMENTS

poem for our winter of Covid-19, "Winter's Tricks", that she wrote in 2017. Anita Spector, a loyal reader of my books and blogs, has given me written permission to publish my response to her poem "Lucky Me" that she wrote for her 80th birthday, and graciously said she feels honored to do so.

Special thanks to Steven Powers, my son-in-law, a painter and Fine Arts Dealer, for his help advising me which images work as a cover and which ones don't, and the design of the final image for three books, including this one.

The Editor-in-Chief of IPBooks, Arnie Richards, gave me encouragement, an unpublished author of senior years, to launch a second career, and Larry and Tamar Schwartz for their patience in guiding me through the process from start to finish.

Also, special thanks to Karen Wescott, a playwright, and actress, and Ute Tellini, a book editor and art historian, who have read and offered to review the book when it is completed. Sadly, a close friend and colleague, Charlie Goodstein, who reviewed several of my books died recently of Covid-19, and I'd like to think he'd have agreed to review this one too. Only Charlie could write of my "hamish personality… that informs but also challenges readers to probe their own set of axioms."

And thanks to:

The first readers of this manuscript, a high school teacher of poetry who prefers to remain anonymous, who commented that it was difficult to follow the organizational plan of the book—how I got from here to there and why I chose to include the poems I did. I was aware of this as a potential problem because I wasn't following a road map or plan. My writing style is more free-associative, traveling the byways, like Holden Caulfield (*The Catcher in the Rye*) who failed out of his third or fourth private school because he digressed when he was supposed to stick to a topic. He explained to his sympathetic teacher, "How do I know what I'm thinking unless I digress? Of course, a book requires a table of contents, a menu for the reader or dinner guests, which I will provide. The second reader agreed and suggested I find a good editor. With the help of Larry and Tamar Schwartz, I found a very good one, Susan Wolf, who provided practical edits (more permissions, public domain poems only or, if not, choose others that are. I sometimes choose a work-around by discussing a poem and suggesting the reader find that poem online.), and perhaps most importantly encouragement to put even more of myself, my reactions to the poems, that she found the most engaging part of the book. I reread the book again, checked for the needed information, deleted extraneous material which put more focus on the many reactions already there; and then, with an evening cocktail in hand, near water, always my muse, I realized what was missing, a list of my favorite poems and why they were my favorites. I imagined a virtual dialogue between author and reader or an actual Zoom session, or two, like a continuous case seminar that was an important part of my psychoanalytic training. I was sitting on my patio with its in-ground fishpond, yellow water lilies in full bloom, bees busy pollinating the flowers, and thought of writing an Afterword, recalling Sabine, my young granddaughter, asking me, "Grandpa, am I your favorite?"

Thank you, Susan Wolf. My editors have been my best teachers.

ACKNOWLEDGMENTS

My thanks to Dr. Edmund Chaitman for the preface.

Since I've thought of a dinner with an extensive menu of appetizers, salads, entrees, and desserts, I'll follow that path. How about starting with an amuse-bouche (the chef's choice to whet your appetite and introduce the meal—like an epigraph) or a knowledgeable waiter to make recommendations (curator, magazine or book editor), a choice of a tasting menu of small portions with some heartier à la carte options and comments on the menu of the origins of the dishes? Or a museum survey exhibit with an orienting essay as to what awaits in each room—another form of tasting menu with an audio guide focusing on especially important works, which you can ignore if you choose because a lesser work catches your eye? Or a really good teacher who loves poetry and teaching and is willing to share with you what she or he is reading—having a conversation about your feelings about the meal or poem—what you're enjoying or doesn't work for you.

CONTENTS

I.
Introduction 1
   Afterwards—Thomas Hardy 1
   Privacy—Robert Pinsky.. 3
   Hidden in the Words is the Poem........................... 4
   Epigraph from Joy Harjo 5
   Epigraph from Matthew Zapruder 7
   To the reader:.. 7
   "My Feet Know the Way" 8

II.
An amuse-bouche: Sabine 11
   Inversa Norway Spruce... 11
   My reading of "Inversa" 12
   Letter to Sabine... 13
   Unreachable—Sabine Bos....................................... 15
   Just Stand Up—Sabine Bos 15
   Campfire—Sabine Bos 16
   Winter's Tricks—Sabine Bos 17
   Addendum for Sabine 18
   Toni Morrison 19

III.
   I Sing My Plain Country Joan—Benjamin Franklin 22
   My Childhood Home I See Again—Abraham Lincoln 25
   The Suicide's Soliloquy 29

IV.
Antiquity: Homer and Virgil 31

V.
Masterpieces of Western Literature and Philosophy 33

VI.
As for Virginia Woolf and *To the Lighthouse* 35
    "the mystery of the thing" 35
    The Charge of the Light Brigade 36
    Alfred Lord Tennyson.. 36

VII.
Why read poetry and how to read poetry 43

VIII.
Anita's poem of gratitude on her 80th birthday 45
    Lucky Me 45
    "An Ode to New Jersey" 48
    "Sonnet 18: Shall I Compare Thee to a Summer's Day?" 49
    William Shakespeare.. 49

IX.
    The Green Lake 51
    Dorothea Lasky 51

X.
On Aging—Cicero 55

XI.
A poem from The New Yorker 57
    From the Catalogue of Cruelty 57
    Donika Kelly.. 57

XII.
    A Haiku to Basho—Maureen Nelson 63

In Kyoto—Basho 64
POETRY OF THE SEVENTEENTH CENTURY— 64
HAIKAI, HAIBUN, KIŌKA 64
The Arrival of Spring—Howard Schwartz......................... 67

XIII.
A change of pace: *The Peanuts Papers* 69
Grief (For Linus Van Pelt)" Part I—Jonathan Lethem........... 70

XIV.
Unnamed—Maureen Nelson 77
The Man in the Moon—Maureen Nelson 78

XV.
An addendum to the Introduction 79
The Love Song of J. Alfred Prufrock—T.S. Eliot 81
I Knew a Woman—Theodore Roethke............................... 87
Running Away Together—Maxine Kumin........................... 88
Looking Back in My Eighty-First Year—Maxine Kumin 93
In the Absence of Bliss—Maxine Kumin 94
The Gift Outright—Robert Frost 100
This Land Is Your Land—Woody Guthrie 101
Stopping by Woods on a Snowy Evening—Robert Frost 102
"Christmas Trees" 104

XVI.
Born to Run—Bruce Springsteen 108
A Poem on the Eve of Impeachment—Frank Bruni............ 109

XVII.
Warm Summer Sun—Mark Twain 114
Annette—Robert Richardson 114
Mark Twain and Sholom Aleichem—Edward Field 118

xix

XVIII.
Books Bound in Red—Marina Tsvetaeva 121

XIX.
The Doctor Stories—William Carlos Williams 126
Dead Baby—William Carlos Williams 128
To Close—William Carlos Williams 129
A Poem After "Notes on the Refrigerator Door"
by William Carlos Williams—Howard Schwartz 130
In Memoriam: William Carlos Williams Note 132

XX.
A Brief Introduction to *Paterson* 133
Epilogue 133
"Asphodel, That Greeny Flower" 134

XXI.
Biography of William Carlos Williams (Wikipedia) 141
What Do You Imagine When You Imagine
Your Life Without Me? 141
Sonnets from the Portuguese 43: "How do I love thee?
Let me count the ways"—Elizabeth Barrett Browning 145
The New Colossus—Emma Lazarus 151
"The Arrival of Spring" 188

XXII.
Poems by Peter Balakian and Howard Schwartz 197
After Zucchini—Peter Balakian 197
Grandma's Hands and Rugelach—Howard Schwartz 199

XXIII.
Poetry is everywhere 203
Ah, Ah—Joy Harjo 204
Break My Heart—Joy Harjo 206

Washing My Mother's Body (pages 30–34) 208
For Those Who Would Govern—Joy Harjo 215

XXIV.

Bless This Land 217
Joy Harjo 217

XXV.

Afterword 221
Unreachable—Sabine Bos 221
Just Stand Up—Sabine Bos 222
The Gettysburg Address—Abraham Lincoln 226
Before and After—Maureen Nelson 230
Unnamed—Maureen Nelson 232
The Man in the Moon 233
In the Absence of Bliss—Maxine Kumin 233
Stopping by Woods on a Snowy Evening—Robert Frost 237
Warm Summer Sun 240
Annette—Robert Richardson 242
Mark Twain and Sholom Aleichem—Edward Field 247

Preface by Edmund Chaitman, M.D.

(Dr. Chaitman is a member of the New Jersey Psychoanalytic Society.)

Of all the statements about the purpose of poetry, Ezra Pound's is the most relevant: "The purpose of poetry is to throw affect on the page."

It was, therefore, no surprise to me on opening Howard Schwartz's *Living with Poetry* to learn that he turned to poetry to help him deal with the feelings stirred by the death of his mother.

Howard is an effective analyst who has spent much of his working life doing what analysts do, helping patients identify their affects, and deal with them effectively.

So, in this volume, Howard continues his analytic work, identifying, clarifying, and sharpening affects. But this time, the analytic work is especially liberating. For rather than dealing with the affects his patients bring to him, he chooses the poets and writes his own poetry, presenting material which is most essential to him.

This collection of poems, taken in its totality, deals with loss, mortality, and (unspoken—as seen most clearly in the coda), the meaning of living a good life.

How does one proceed to build a new life, one poet asks, weighed down by memories in their pockets? Dr. Schwartz's answer involves friends, family, and "Just Stand Up." by Sabine Bos, his granddaughter.

"Just Stand Up" is a statement of both accepting affects and, more importantly, a call to move forward. This call to action and the dangers of the inhibited, unlived life are the themes of my own favorite poem: T.S. Eliot's "The Love Song of J. Alfred Prufrock."

Prufrock bemoans the fact that he did not "stand up." Instead, hampered by a hundred decisions and indecisions, does he dare to eat a peach?

He has measured out his life in coffee spoons. How much better had he been "a pair of ragged claws scuttling across the floor of the seas."

I was astounded to learn, many years after reading Prufrock in Freshman English, that Eliot was only 23 when he wrote the poem. The cause of such despair in a young man, I do not know.

But we do know Sabine and Schwartz's remedy as suggested in the coda: Edward Field's "Mark Twain and Sholem Aleichem." After a little good-natured (and I think essentially Jewish) ribbing, the two men, near the end of their lives, cavort in the sea (echoing Eliot's claws in the sea), laughing and living life to the fullest.

I believe Howard has lived his life to the fullest, and this volume may help others to cavort with Mark Twain and Sholem Aleichem. If you do, you will not be in bad company.

I.
Introduction

Several months ago, I began reading poetry, ten minutes every night from an anthology *An Invitation to Poetry*, edited by Robert Pinsky—Poet Laureate of the US 1997-2000—who founded the Favorite Poem Project with Maggie Dietz, the director of the Favorite Poem Project. I bought this book of 200 poems on a whim, attracted to it by a DVD with a video introduction by Robert Pinsky.

The opening flap of the cover of the book announces: "For readers unaccustomed to reading poetry, this anthology offers illuminating examples of the infinitely various ways a poem reaches a reader."

An example that moved me:

When asked to write an introduction to a book written by a colleague who had recently died whose publisher is the same as mine, I came upon Thomas Hardy, England (1840-1928). It was chosen by a reader who "finds it is the ultimate Eulogy for that person who treasures and appreciates life in our natural world."— Virginia Brady, Plattsburg, NY

Afterwards
Thomas Hardy

When the Present latched its postern behind my tremulous stay.
And the May Month flaps its glad green wings like wings

Delicate-filmed as new-spun silk, will the neighbors say,
"He was a man who noticed such things?"

If it be in the dusk when, like an eyelid's soundless blink
The dewfall-hawk comes crossing the shades to alight
Upon the wind-warped upland thorn, a gazer may think,
"to him this must have been a familiar sign.

If I pass during some nocturnal blackness, mothy and warm,
When the hedgehog travels furtively over the lawn,
One may say, "He strove that such innocent creatures should
Come to no harm.
But he could do little for them; and now he is gone."

If when hearing that I have been stilled at last, they stand at the door,
Watching the full-starred heavens that winter sees'
Will this thought rise on those,
"He was one who had an eye for such mysteries"?

And will any say when my bell of quittance is heard in the gloom,
And a crossing breeze cuts a pause in its outpolling's,
Till they rise again, as they were a new bell's boom
"He hears it not now, but used to notice such things"?

Browsing the book, I found at least a half dozen or more poems that were meaningful to me for various reasons, which demonstrate the value of Pinsky's introduction to poetry. But then I realized I've been reading poetry without thinking about it for a long time, but none written by Robert Pinsky until I read "Privacy" in the *New York Times*, 1/3/20,

Privacy
Robert Pinsky

In the World War some say has never ended
He waited for his train. The cold of Hell.
The overcrowded Terminal stank and rumbled.

Each week, a new law to amuse the public.
("Jews are no longer permitted to own a cat.")
On the marble stairs, a colony of beggars.

What was the word, he wondered, for what he saw
That stung like a curdled cinder in his eye:
A peasant family spread their cloth on the floor.

Their mismatched floral crockery. Bread and tea.
Overhead speakers roaring propaganda.
Syntax of gestures, handing a child a cup.

They likely were illiterate, he thinks,
Still wondering as an old man in America.
Once, teaching a slave to read was against the law.

Yet sometimes it happened, covertly or in the open.
Does the online Form conceal an overcrowding?
Some of us click the box "Declines to Answer."

Thinking in his mother tongue he recalls the loaf
They carved, that formal alphabet of custom
In the soiled Station, public but somehow private.

Robert Pinsky was the United States poet laureate from 1997 to 2000.

Hidden in the Words is the Poem

We begin to see that all they want to tell us and have failed to communicate is the poem, the poem which their lives are being lived to realize.

From William Carlos Williams, *The Doctor Stories*

An introduction that expresses my intentions and aspirations better than I could.[2]

"Do we not see we are inarticulate? This is what defeats us. It is our inability to communicate with another how we are locked within ourselves, unable to say the simplest thing of importance to another... that gives the physician. . .a wonderful opportunity actually to watch the words being born... But after we have run through the gamut of simple meanings that come to one over the years a change gradually occurs... And then a new meaning begins to intervene. For under that language to which we have been listening all our lives a new, a more profound language, a new language underlying all the dialectics offers itself. It is what they call poetry. That is the final phase. It is that we realize, which is beyond all they have been saying is what they have been trying to say...We begin to see that all they want to tell us and have failed to communicate is the poem, the poem which their lives are being lived to realize. No one will believe it.

---

2   Williams, W.C. (1932). *The Doctor Stories*. New York: New Directions Press, pages 124–125.

And it is the actual words, as we hear them spoken under all circumstances which contain it. It is actually there, in the life before us, every minute that we are listening… which is hidden in the very words from which we must recover underlying meanings as realistically as we must recover metal out of ore…..And it is our very life. It is we ourselves at our rarest moments, but inarticulate for the most part, except one man every five or six hundred years, escapes to formulate a few gifted sentences."

And from the 2020 Poet Laureate and author of *An American Sunrise* Joy Harjo[3]:

"Don't worry about what a poem means. Do you ask what a song means before you listen? Just listen."—Joy Harjo

Epigraph from Joy Harjo
Poet Laureate of United States 2019
An American Sunrise

"You cannot force poetry
With a ruler or jail it at a desk.
Mystery is blind, but wills you
To untie the cloth, in eternity."

---

3   Harjo, J. (2019). *An American Sunrise*. New York: W.W. Norton & Company.

Epigraph from Matthew Zapruder
Author of *Why Poetry*

"The usefulness of poetry has less to do with delivering a "message (which we can just easily get from prose), and far more to do with what poems can easily do to our language, reinventing it and reactivating it, and thereby drawing us into a different form of attention and awareness."

To the reader:

Let's take a break to consider whether my 'enthusiasm needs to be curbed' (Larry David, the coproducer and writer for Jerry Seinfeld's iconic TV sitcom and the show *Curb Your Enthusiasm*, wasn't for everyone.) I've read many more poems than appear in this book because I've become a reader of poetry, which I didn't much favor—although exposed to it in college, Shakespeare, Dante, Homer, and Virgil—until I started to read poetry now (sixty years later), listened to poets read and discuss their work on public radio and YouTube videos—the idea of attending a poetry reading never occurred to me in college or after. I've learned that to truly appreciate poetry, it's best to read it out loud to hear the rhythm of the words, not to rush or perhaps to rush when the words drive you on—Tennyson's *The Charge of the Light Brigade*. The poem I wrote after my mother's death, August 21, 1966, is a slow journey, not to be rushed, that still brings tears to my eyes, as I hear myself speak it.

"My Feet Know the Way"

I wrote this prose poem after my mother's death at age 84—Aug 21, 1966—and it is in most of my books, most recently in *Women: Biology, Culture, and Literature* (IP Books, 2019).

Today is a warm and bright Indian Summer day, like those that so often ease prayers for a healthy New Year, a Wednesday not unlike that Tuesday of terror and death three years ago.

There is little traffic as I exit the Lincoln Tunnel and drive east across 34th Street to the Queens Midtown Tunnel. Shouldn't I have turned north and then east through Central Park at 65th Street and then north again on Madison Avenue to 87th Street to pick up my mother for our yearly visit to Mt. Hebron Cemetery? That is where I am going this Wednesday of the year 5765, but my mother no longer lives at 110 East 87th Street. She cannot greet me with a smile and a kiss, her Union Prayer Book in hand. She is buried in Mt. Hebron with my father and her parents and two of her siblings and her nephew and her sister-in-law and my father's siblings and his mother—loved by him but not by my mother.

Our last visit to this final resting place in Queens for tens of thousands of strangers with familiar, comforting Jewish names was in 1995. The monuments of those strangers always reassured me that if they were "Devoted-Loving-Caring" husbands, wives, parents, grandparents, and siblings and friends, to be remembered, engraved in stone, for all time that way, then so could I live to be remembered like them. In death our failings are forgiven. Their monuments give testimony to the compassion of the living.

How ironic that this Wednesday I park not ten feet from the Main Street entrance gate. That last visit with my mother I parked a long half block away from that gate. We'd chatted, as always, on the drive across the Triboro Bridge, past LaGuardia Airport and east unto the Long Island Expressway for one mile until exiting at Main Street in Queens. A right turn at the first light leads to Mt. Hebron. These travel directions are not to be forgotten for they lead to treasure. That Wednesday my mother looked well, but she was not well. Why didn't I drop her off at the gate? She was not fully recovered from several recent heart attacks and was already losing vision from a growing pituitary tumor. Was I callous and inconsiderate? Or did I selfishly need her to be well and strong? She'd always loved walking, and so I let her walk. Past the gate, we turned right on the first path toward the far boundary fence. She carried her prayer book in which she'd written the Hebrew names and the dates of death of those we would visit. Also written in her clutched book were the names of the living, mine and my brother's, Chaim Baer and Schmuel Avrum ben David (my father's name). Surely, she never thought she'd outlive us. Perhaps we were to be with her as she walked these paths of remembrance? In her book was a time-creased map with an x at the block and lot of each gravesite (her treasure map). We never looked at that map.

Our feet knew the way.

That day my mother stumbled and fell. I joked as I helped her up, "It's not your time to lie on this ground." She laughed, but maybe we both knew her remaining time on this earth was short. We would not walk together this way again.

Today I am alone as I visit my aunt Shari and her son, George, my uncle Louie and his wife Gertie, my grandma Malvina, she of the white hair and beautiful hands into whose protection I ran when pursued at times by my angry mother, and her husband Morris, a grandfather I never knew. I remember and place two stones on their graves, for while alone I am not alone. My mother is with me still.

I walk more slowly to my parents' graves, aware that my walking companion could no longer walk at a march. How strange to feel I am walking with her to visit her grave. I sit on the unadorned bench before their simple monument, both designed by my brother in minimalist style, and speak to my parents. I recite the Kaddish. I become aware that a fig tree I planted this past summer was a healing gesture of love for my father. He had planted plum, apricot, and peach trees in our Grumman Avenue yard. We had longingly admired a pear tree we passed each fall as we walked familiar streets to Young Israel Synagogue for Rosh Hashanah and Yom Kippur services. I forgive myself for my impatience and anger with him. I loved him and think I have become like him. He died in 1966, and today I cried at his grave.

At the far fence, past my parents' graves, lie Rose, Viola, Armin, Pauline, Aaron, Samuel, Morris and Hanna, my fathers' siblings, in-laws, and mother. My childhood lies before me, and on each monument, I place two stones (except for his mother's, who was jealous and never accepted my mother).

My parents were my twin towers. They dug my foundations deep, and now there is a hole in the sky above me where they once stood. I stand and they are fallen. Today Sue is buying a burial plot for us in Beth David Cemetery in Kenilworth near the graves of her parents. I will rest with her, as is right; but today I think I will miss Mt. Hebron. My feet know the way here. When I no longer walk these paths who will visit and place stones, say Kaddish, and remember?

As I approach the Main Street gate a middle-aged woman and her white-haired mother enter the cemetery. I nod, "Hello," but they are talking and do not acknowledge me. They are not looking at a map. Their feet know the way.

II.
An amuse-bouche: Sabine

Sabine, my granddaughter, was an accomplished and published poet (*Scholastic*) when she wrote "Inversa" at age sixteen while visiting the Smith College campus, on a lawn surrounded by large spruce trees, including the Picea Abies 'Inversa' Weeping Norway Spruce.

Inversa Norway Spruce
Sabine Bos

In a garden he wanders
aimless.
The brush,
timid,
grazing his ankles
as sunlight seeps into his shriveled surface.

Amidst delicate flowers,
perfectly pristine,
ripe and vibrant with color,

he sees himself.
In the upward and down again sloping trunk
(a reflection of the curve of his back.

In the tenacious grip of the bark onto its skeleton
(like his skin, a mosaic of
tangled creases,
the last line of defense
before the years infect his bones
and guide them to decay).

Its limbs extend outward, yet
its fingertips barely reach
the brush it shades.

Out of touch
(just the way his trembling fingers
are unable to grasp a memory,
just the way his childhood eludes him).

Larger trees, confidently rooted,
thieves of the weeping old man's sun,
plunge him
into the damp, bitter air.

My reading of "Inversa"

I've struggled to understand "Inversa" and then did my best to help her parents understand it when they asked for my help, not as a teacher who never took a poetry course, but as a reader now learning how to read and listen to poetry by a master teacher—*Why Poetry* by Matthew Zapruder—and by speaking out loud the poems I've begun to read. In the Introduction, Zapruder wrote "This book was written not to give all the answers... but to be a starting point. Reading it should make it more possible for anyone to find the poems that matter to them. Most of all, I hoped that when I was finished with this book, whenever anyone told me they don't know how to read poetry, I could hand them this book and say, I believe just by being alive you already do."

Letter to Sabine

I read "Inversa" four times—and then out loud—before it dawned on me you were reflecting on human life (Inverse: opposite or contrary in position, direction, order, or effect: Webster's Dictionary). Your metaphor of the long-lived Norwegian Spruce, which grows tall, but also the inverse, low and weeping, was abundant on the Smith campus where you visited last summer, stirred your feelings about the short-lived life of man—metaphors are the heart of poetry. Maybe it took me so long to grasp your meaning because at age eighty it was hard to grasp that you at age sixteen were so sensitively aware of mortality—the tree is an old man, an individual man is 'mankind'—as well as literally your aging grandparents, and still young but also aging parents. Last year both of your Dad's parents died, so the poem is perhaps also a eulogy for them and a form of mourning as well.

The tall tree blocks the light of the smaller as it reaches for the sky, as the bent back of man descends to (into) the earth. Many years ago, Grandma and I hiked in the Grand Tetons in Wyoming through a burned-out forest recovering from a fire caused by lightning. The young shoots were sprouting because the fire was necessary to release the spores protecting the seeds in the earth. It was exciting to see the continuity of life that requires death.

As for memory as a function of life, I couldn't agree more that as we age, our backs bent, and our skin wrinkled and mottled, that memory of our youth may fade (a word, or date, or name or the identity of a loved one or even our own name), but it is not inevitable. Someday medical researchers may find a biologic means to arrest or cure the process. They are reaching for the (tall) spruce—what another apt metaphor for your poem. But your ending is gloomy, and I wonder why? I am aging and so is Grandma, but we are not weeping and bitter, nor are most of our friends who are older than us, eighty-five or seven. Most have serious hobbies, and some like me continue to work or have a second career, as do I as a writer. A world-famous psychologist, Erik Erikson (now deceased), who taught at Harvard for many years, wrote a book in his 90s, *Vital Involvement in Old Age*, warning us to prepare for aging by becoming as wise as our mental capacity and our character allows so we can contribute to the strivings of youth. The philosopher Cicero, (44 BC), in a short dialogue on the joys of one's advanced years called *On Old Age*, wrote that he could no longer lead men into battle—your 'weeping spruce'—but he could remain vital as a counselor, teacher, writer, or poet to those "strong, straight and tall Norway spruces reaching for the sky."

One last comment. I thought there was no word 'inversa' until I Googled for an image of the Smith College Campus and discovered the tree that inspired your poem in the arboretum.

Richard Cohen, author of *How to Write Like Tolstoy: A Journey into the Minds of our Greatest Writers,* recommends book titles and first sentences be "grabbers"—to draw you right in. "Inversa Norway Spruce" is a grabber.

Sabine is to this day shy, but her poetry is anything but:

Unreachable
Sabine Bos

I am strewn like a blanket upon the universe
I dive headfirst into grass and my fingers graze disaster
I compete with hope and I demolish sanity.
I thrive and flourish in the hearts of the weak
In the darkness I march triumphantly
My gun has unlimited ammunition
I am the immortal plant
A seed from within
Until I grow
I grow and I possess
I crank the gears of the mind
I tug and expose the impossible scenarios
Until imagination cracks from the pressure
I cannot be received for I am long gone
I am unreachable
I am fear

Just Stand Up
Sabine Bos

What's there to see with your eyes opened but your mind closed off
You feel to touch but not to impose
What is a gift if you don't receive it
A candle is there but it isn't lit
Open your mind and don't close the door
You will be exposed to so much more
No steps back, keep running forwards

Knowledge is dangerous
A sharp precise sword
Don't open your mouth to say nothing at all
Respond to nobody's beck and call
You are yourself and no one else
A thick unique book on a shelf
Don't rip out the pages
Acknowledge the thought
It's a lesson that must be eternally taught
Questions directions they cut
Don't let them catch you
Just stand up

And she writes sweetly but strongly without irony:

Campfire
Sabine Bos

Sway with the rhythmic strum of the guitar
Drape your arms around one another
Create unity amongst strangers
Feel the subtle but persistent heat of the contained flames
Sing along even if the words are unknown
Jump when the sparks make the sharp welcoming crack
Let your smile infect those around you
Your personality roams free when surrounded by liberated minds
Embrace the together

And a poem which reminds us of our fragility before the power of nature, ironically apt to this winter of Covid-19.

Winter's Tricks
Scholastic Key Award, 2017
Sabine Bos

I forget
what the sun looks like
Summer left us
longer ago than I can remember
Winter called her back
to captivity
The soft breeze finally let down
its idly fabricated visage
and returned to a cruel and icy
Wind
Biting our skin with its sharp and
unrelenting canines
painting our skin
the sickly color of paper
Feeding us thoughts laced with venom and sinking us
far into the earth
so that we are gasping for air
Winter loves proving just
how strong gravity truly is
She justifies her brutal abuse
by growing flowers
in the spring, speckling the world
with perfect picturesque
pockets of color
By liberating the sun from its cage
By letting it warm our skin
and our souls for

a few fleeting, glorious moments
We rejoice in its brilliance
and dance in the light
like children
Little do we know
that while we allow smiles
to wash our faces
To cleanse them
of endless layers of dirt and ash
The heat is frying our skin because
we are fragile
And we can only bask
in the sun's warm embrace for so long
before we burn.

Addendum for Sabine

For Hanukkah, Sabine asked for poems by Toni Morrison, whose novels she had been reading. Unfortunately, a book of five poems Toni Morrison published is no longer available, although one of those poems appears in her Pulitzer Prizewinning novel *Beloved:*

Stunned and grieved by Toni Morrison's death (Aug 6, 2019), the Beverly Rogers, Carol C. Harter Black Mountain Institute, home of *The Believer*, is reckoning with its own humble encounter with this towering figure in modern letters. In 2002, Morrison offered five original poems for a limited-edition, letterpress book to help fund the institute's work advancing freedom of expression. According to the scholar Stephanie Li, these poems "represent Morrison's first and only foray into verse." What makes the book—produced by the printer Peter Koch in an edition of 399 numbered copies and 26 lettered copies—all the more remarkable is the inclusion of silhouettes by Kara Walker in response to Morrison's poems. "The partnership between Morrison and Walker," Li writes, "is both remarkable and unprecedented. Although Walker has cited Morrison as a key influence on her artistic development and critics have begun to analyze intersections in their work, *Five Poems* is the first demonstration of collaboration" between them.

The series Morrison contributed to also includes letterpress books with contributions from Salman Rushdie, Joyce Carol Oates, Kenzaburo Oe, and Wole Soyinka, among others, each with its own vivid history. But none can match the publication of the only poetry known to have been authored by Toni Morrison."—Joshua Wolf Shenk, Editor-in-Chief, *The Believer* magazine

It's as if she knows who she is and that, in that knowing, her declarations here will live forever.—Jericho Brown, Poetry Editor, *The Believer* magazine

However, Sabine was very pleased with a boxed set of novels, *Beloved*, *Song of Solomon*, and *The Bluest Eye*—she had not read The Bluest Eye but planned to read the others again as well.

Toni Morrison

This morning in the *New York Times Magazine* Section (Dec. 29, 2019) *THE LIVES THEY LIVED* appeared: a Toni Morrison poem for Sabine:

In 1993, Toni Morrison won the Nobel Prize in Literature, becoming the first black woman to ever to do so. Her friend the poet Sonia Sanchez, a Professor of English at Temple University for 20 years, was the one to deliver the news.

"I turned on the idiot box, and it was the overseas news and it said, Toni Morrison has won the Nobel Prize in Literature'. I picked up the phone and dialed Sister Toni at Princeton. 'Toni, Toni, Toni, you won the Nobel Prize in Literature. 'She said—and I quote— 'Have you been drinking? I ignored that, I said, 'Maybe you should turn your television on.' There was a silence, and then she said, 'Well I guess we have to think about the most important things to do.' 'What is that?' 'Figure out what we're going to wear.' I would teach Sister Toni and students would say, "It's so hard. Her work is not easy to read. I finally told them to read her work out loud and you'll understand it.[4] One just used to stare at me when I said it, but she's a poet in disguise as a novelist. If you read her work as a poem, you will understand it. You don't understand every word or every image in a poem, but you get the context of it, the fullness. 'And the same thing is true with Ms. Morrison,' I said. When you read her, it's like discovering texts you had never read before. It's almost like you were excavating some place in Africa, and opened a tomb, and in that tomb were all of the stories that we should have known, all of our stories of our enslavement in this country, all of her story and history of us came up like a breath."

---

4   I didn't realize until this was re-read, as suggested by Susan Wolf, that this was the source of the title to this book, nor did I do a plagiarism check. Thank you, Sonia Sanchez, Professor of English at Temple University. Since I wrote this footnote, the title of the book has been changed to *Living with Poetry: Finding Something Deep Inside Yourself That Only Poetry Can Reach.*

III.

For a change of pace, let's consider Benjamin Franklin and Abraham Lincoln.

"I Sing My Plain Country Joan" 1742

American Philosophical Society

There can be little doubt that Franklin composed these verses to his wife. They are assigned to him in two different anecdotes, which, though the incidents described are separated by forty years, are not inconsistent. The first, from the family of Franklin's friend John Bard, relates how, at a meeting of some club, possibly the Junto, someone jokingly took exception to the practice of married men singing songs poets had written in praise of their mistresses. Next morning, Dr. Bard, who had been in one of the companies and may have been the expostulator, received the following song from Franklin, with a request that he be ready to sing it at the next meeting. The second anecdote was conveyed to a London magazine by one John Ellis, Jr., in 1807. Franklin was one of the guests at a dinner in Paris at which each person was to compose verses in praise of a wife. When his turn came, Franklin had ready this song. He subsequently gave a copy to a woman friend and told her the circumstances; and she gave them to Ellis to publish.

Franklin himself provided further evidence of his connection with the song. Writing in a playful vein to Catharine Ray, September 11, 1755, he informed her that Deborah Franklin "talks of bequeathing me to you as a Legacy; But I ought to wish you a better, and hope she will live these 100 Years; for we are grown old together, and if she has any faults, I am so us'd to 'em that I don't perceive 'em, as the Song says," and he quoted the stanza here inserted next to the last.

Finally, the manuscript from which the song is printed, though not in Franklin's hand, certainly belonged to him. It is preserved among his papers, and Deborah has written on the back of one sheet a note of charges to an unknown customer at the New Printing-Office—8d. for an almanac, for example. Carl Van Doren printed the verses without assigning a date, though he mentions that Bard moved from Philadelphia in 1746. If Franklin's "plain Country Joan" was Deborah, the reference to twelve years of marriage would fix the date of composition at about 1742.

I Sing My Plain Country Joan
Benjamin Franklin

Of their Chloes and Phillisses Poets may prate
I sing my plain Country Joan
Now twelve Years my Wife, still the Joy of my Life
Blest Day that I made her my own,
My dear Friends
Blest Day that I made her my own.

2
Not a Word of her Face, her Shape, or her Eyes,
Of Flames or of Darts shall you hear;
Tho' I Beauty admire 'tis Virtue I prize,
That fades not in seventy Years,

My dear Friends

3
In Health a Companion delightfull and dear,
Still easy, engaging, and Free,
In Sickness no less than the faithfullest Nurse
As tender as tender can be,
My dear Friends

4
In Peace and good Order, my Houshold she keeps
Right Careful to save what I gain
Yet chearfully spends, and smiles on the Friends
I've the Pleasures to entertain
My dear Friends

5
She defends my good Name ever where I'm to blame,
Friend firmer was ne'er to Man giv'n,
Her compassionate Breast, feels for all the Distrest,
Which draws down the Blessing from Heav'n,
My dear Friends

6
Am I laden with Care, she takes off a large Share,
That the Burthen ne'er makes [me] to reel,
Does good Fortune arrive, the Joy of my Wife,
Quite doubles the Pleasures I feel,
My dear Friends

7
In Raptures the giddy Rake talks of his Fair,
Enjoyment shall make him Despise,
I speak my cool sence, that long Experience,
And Enjoyment have chang'd in no wise,
My dear Friends
[Some Faults we have all, and so may my Joan,
But then they're exceedingly small;
And now I'm us'd to 'em, they're just like my own,
I scarcely can see 'em at all,
My dear Friends,
I scarcely can see them at all.]

8
Were the fairest young Princess, with Million in Purse
To be had in Exchange for my Joan,
She could not be a better Wife, nought be a Worse,
So I'd stick to my Joggy1 alone
My dear Friends
I'd cling to my lovely could Joan

Abraham Lincoln

Abraham Lincoln, who Robert Pinsky considered the "real thing," shared many poems with his friend Andrew Johnson, including "My Childhood Home I See Again" (Poetry.org-Public Domain) and "The Suicide's Soliloquy", Aug 25, 1838. (Wikipedia).

My Childhood Home I See Again
Abraham Lincoln

My childhood's home I see again,
And sadden with the view;
And still, as memory crowds my brain,
There's pleasure in it too.

O Memory! thou midway world
'Twixt earth and paradise,
Where things decayed and loved ones lost
In dreamy shadows rise,

And, freed from all that's earthly vile,
Seem hallowed, pure, and bright,
Like scenes in some enchanted isle
All bathed in liquid light.

As dusky mountains please the eye
When twilight chases day;
As bugle-tones that, passing by,
In distance die away;

As leaving some grand waterfall,
We, lingering, list its roar--
So memory will allow all
We've known, but know no more.

Near twenty years have passed away
Since here I bid farewell

To woods and fields, and scenes of play,
And playmates loved so well.

Where many were, but few remain
Of old familiar things;
But seeing them, to mind again
The lost and absent brings.
The friends left that parting day,
How changed, as time has sped!
Young childhood grown, strong manhood gray,
And half of all are dead.

I hear the loved survivors tell
How naught from death could save,
Till every sound appears a knell,
And every spot a grave.

I range the fields with pensive tread,
And pace the hollow rooms,
And feel (companion of the dead)
I'm living in the tombs.

But here's an object more of dread
Than ought the grave contains--
A human form with reason fled,
While wretched life remains.

Poor Matthew! Once of genius bright,
A fortune-favored child--
Now locked for aye, in mental night,
A haggard mad-man wild.

Poor Matthew! I have ne'er forgot,
When first, with maddened will,
Yourself you maimed, your father fought,
And mother strove to kill;

When terror spread, and neighbors ran,
Your dangerous strength to bind;
And soon, a howling crazy man
Your limbs were fast confined.

How then you strove and shrieked aloud,
Your bones and sinews bared;
And fiendish on the gazing crowd,
With burning eye-balls glared--

And begged, and swore, and wept and prayed
With maniac laughter joined--
How fearful were those signs displayed
By pangs that killed thy mind!

And when at length, tho' drear and long,
Time smoothed thy fiercer woes,
How plaintively thy mournful song
Upon the still night rose.

I've heard it oft, as if I dreamed,
Far distant, sweet, and lone--
The funeral dirge, it ever seemed
Of reason dead and gone.

To drink its strains, I've stole away,
All stealthily and still,
Ere yet the rising God of day
Had streaked the Eastern hill.

Air held his breath; trees, with the spell,
Seemed sorrowing angels round,
Whose swelling tears in dew-drops fell
Upon the listening ground.

But this is past; and naught remains,
That raised thee o'er the brute.
Thy piercing shrieks, and soothing strains,
Are like, forever mute.

Now fare thee well—more thou the cause,
Than subject now of woe.
All mental pangs, by time's kind laws,
Hast lost the power to know.

O death! Thou awe-inspiring prince,
That keeps the world in fear;
Why dost those tear more blest ones hence,
And leave him ling 'ring here.

The Suicide's Soliloquy

An unsigned poem, likely written by Abraham Lincoln, first published on August 25, 1838, in *The Sangamo Journal,* in Springfield, Illinois.

Shortly after Lincoln's assassination, one of Lincoln's personal friends, Joshua Speed, told William Herndon, Lincoln's biographer, that Lincoln had written and published "a few lines under the gloomy title of Suicide." No one had found the actual article. In 1997, independent writer Richard Lawrence Miller found "The Suicide's Soliloquy" and, in 2002, came to realize that it matched the descriptions of Lincoln's missing article. Although it seems to follow the same themes and style as Lincoln›s other works, there is still controversy over whether it was actually written by Lincoln.

The following lines were said to have been found near the bones of a man supposed to have committed suicide, in a deep forest, on the flat branch of the Sangamon, some time ago.

The Suicide's Soliloquy

Here, where the lonely hooting owl
Sends forth his midnight moans,
Fierce wolves shall o'er my carcass growl,
Or buzzards pick my bones.

No fellow-man shall learn my fate,
Or where my ashes lie;
Unless by beasts drawn round their bait,
Or by the ravens' cry.

Yes! I've resolved the deed to do,
And this the place to do it:
This heart I'll rush a dagger through,
Though I in hell should rue it!

Hell! What is hell to one like me
Who pleasures never knew;
By friends consigned to misery,
By hope deserted too?

To ease me of this power to think,
That through my bosom raves,
I'll headlong leap from hell's high brink,
And wallow in its waves.

Though devils yell, and burning chains
May waken long regret;
Their frightful screams, and piercing pains,
Will help me to forget.

Yes! I'm prepared, through endless night,
To take that fiery berth!
Think not with tales of hell to fright
Me, who am damn'd on earth!

Sweet steel! come forth from your sheath,
And glist'ning, speak your powers;
Rip up the organs of my breath,
And draw my blood in showers!

I strike! It quivers in that heart
Which drives me to this end;
I draw and kiss the bloody dart,
My last—my only friend.

IV.

Antiquity: Homer and Virgil

The reunion of Ulysses and Penelope—*the Odyssey*[5]

*A*nd *as when the land appears welcome to men who are swimming, after Poseidon has smashed their strong-built ships on the open water, pounding it with the weight of wind and the heavy seas, and only a few escape the gray water landward by swimming with a thick scurf of salt coated upon them, and gladly they set foot upon the shore, escaping the evil; so welcome was her husband to her as she looked upon him, and she would not let him go from the embrace of her white arms. Now Dawn of the rosy fingers would have dawned on their weeping, had not the grey-eyed goddess Athena planned it otherwise. She held the long night back at the outward edge, she detained Dawn of the golden throne by the Ocean and would not let her harness her fast-footed horses who bring the daylight to people: Lampos and Phaeton, the Dawn's horses, who carry her.... Then resourceful Odysseus spoke to his wife, saying: 'Dear wife, we have not yet come to the limit of all our trials....*

5

I know I read Virgil's *The Aeneid* in college, but I can't recall anything about it. What comes to mind was a saying from *The Aeneid* at the 9/11 Memorial, controversial in its usage but powerful to me:

"No day shall erase you from the memory of time."
From end to end, the sentence stretches 60 feet.

The memorial inscription (translated), "No day shall erase you from the memory of time" is an eloquent translation of the original Latin of *The Aeneid*—"Nulla dies umquam memori vos eximet aevo."

Personal note: My last view of the Twin Towers was from a 37-foot sloop. I was sailing south from the Verrazano Bridge on a sunset sail with the setting sun illuminating the Twin Towers to the east. It was several years before I could bear to visit the Memorial and its message—"No day shall erase you from the memory of time."

What began as a digression into Space and the terrors of 9/11 led me back to the Literature Humanities Core Curriculum to see what it looks like today.

Clearly, I've been inspired by Sabine's poems. Sad to say, I can't recall ever being taught poetry in high school[6]. It was part of the Core Curriculum (Virgil, Shakespeare, Dante, Cervantes, and Goethe) at Columbia C'59.

---

6   Schwartz, H. (2017) *Hide and Seek/Hidden and Found – In search of a Balanced Life-Psychoanalytic Memoirs, Stories and Essays.* New York: IPBooks, page 107.

V.
Masterpieces of Western Literature and Philosophy

Humanities A has been part of the Core Curriculum of Columbia College for seventy-five years. Some titles have never left the required reading list: Homer, *The Iliad;* Aeschylus, *Oresteia;* and Dante, *The Inferno*. Others have rotated on and off. Today's Literature Humanities includes works ranging from *The Holy Bible* and Augustine's *Confessions* to Montaigne's *Essays* and Virginia Woolf's *To the Lighthouse. I would feel right at home because I have read Montaigne and had a short piece published in the New York Times, and written at length about Virginia Woolf's To the Lighthouse.*

Re: *Ghosts in the Machine* to the *New York Times 12/27/2015*

"Before there was Facebook, Michel de Montaigne published his *Essays* on March 1, 1580. In his Introduction, he wrote: 'To the reader (intending it for his relatives and friends) ... so that when they have lost me—which they soon must—they may recover some features of my character and disposition, and thus keep the memory of me more completely and vividly alive.' In this age of instant communication with countless friends and digital mourning, how many of us remember and honor the character of this reclusive reader and writer who retired to his library at age 47 to "try on ideas for himself and others—*essai* is the French word for trial—and created the Essay. The entire book is a delight and a good read for 2016. My favorites are: On the education of children, On the power of imagination, and On presumption.

Howard Schwartz, MD,
Columbia College, C'59

VI.
As for Virginia Woolf and *To the Lighthouse*[7]

Ah, the mystery of the thing—Virginia Woolf

"the mystery of the thing"

Really, there is no mystery. Woolf is like a mystery writer who announces at the start who dun it. The mystery is the why and how they do it, and in certain mysteries why they keep doing it over and over again. The opening pages tell us that Mr. Ramsey is planning a trip to the lighthouse that James, his six-year-old son, has been looking forward to for years. It involves sailing several miles over open sea to a spit of land on dangerous rocks on which many ships have foundered. James is a sensitive boy whose nature is to fix on the joys or sorrows of the moment. He is distracting himself while he awaits the news about the weather, while his mother, tenderly watching, sees him in the future "on the Bench or directing a stern and momentous enterprise in some crisis of public affairs (like her—the author's—father who she worshipped but died when she was twenty-two years old and after her mother's death when she was thirteen years old.) Mr. R. announces, "But it won't be fine." "There

---

7   Woolf, V. *To the Lighthouse*. (1994). Wordsworth Classics, West Hertfordshire, England: Wordsworth Classics.

35

and then had there been an axe handy or any weapon that would have gashed a hole in his father's breast James would have seized it... by his mere presence... lean as a knife, narrow as the blade of one, grinning sarcastically and casting ridicule on his wife... what he said was true. (It was dangerous that morning.) He was incapable of untruth and (rationalized) his cruelty as a lesson that life holds many disappointments and they (his children) must learn to endure.

'But it may be fine—I expect it will be fine, as she knitted a sock for the Lighthouse keeper to give to his little boy."

There you have it. Versions of this scenario recur as a leitmotif and make the point that her husband and she must create a new dynamic—not just for themselves but for their children. too. Woolf makes her point not didactically but by allusion.

Mr. Ramsey's mantra is:

The Charge of the Light Brigade
Alfred Lord Tennyson

Half a league, half a league,
Flashed all their sabres bare,
Flashed as they turned in air
Sabring the gunners there,
Charging an army, while
All the world wondered.
Plunged in the battery-smoke
Right through the line they broke;
Cossack and Russian
Reeled from the sabre stroke

Shattered and sundered.
Then they rode back, but not
Not the six hundred.

II

"Forward, the Light Brigade!"
Was there a man dismayed?
Not though the soldier knew
  Someone had blundered.
Theirs not to make reply,
Theirs not to reason why,
Theirs but to do and die.
Into the valley of Death
  Rode the six hundred.

III

Cannon to right of them,
Cannon to left of them,
Cannon in front of them
  Volleyed and thundered;
Stormed at with shot and shell,
Boldly they rode and well,
Into the jaws of Death,
Into the mouth of hell
  Rode the six hundred.

IV

Flashed all their sabres bare,
Flashed as they turned in air
Sabring the gunners there,
Charging an army, while

All the world wondered.
Plunged in the battery-smoke
Right through the line they broke;
Cossack and Russian
Reeled from the sabre stroke
Shattered and sundered.
Then they rode back, but not
Not the six hundred.

V

Cannon to right of them,
Cannon to left of them,
Cannon behind them
Volleyed and thundered;
Stormed at with shot and shell,
While horse and hero fell.
They that had fought so well
Came through the jaws of Death,
Back from the mouth of hell,
All that was left of them,
Left of six hundred.

VI

When can their glory fade?
O the wild charge they made!
All the world wondered.
Honour the charge they made!
Honour the Light Brigade,
Noble six hundred!

Mrs. R. reads a story to James, who she recognizes as a kindred spirit, a sad, ironic Grimm's fairy tale: A poor fisherman catches and releases a 'Golden Flounder,' a prince in disguise. His wife nags him to ask the fish for ever greater rewards until the Golden Flounder returns them to their original poverty. This is indeed a strange tale to read to James and cries for interpretation:

Children sense dysfunction in a family, and James knows that his dad is not the prince his mom thought she married. She can't nag him to be who he is not and is punished for wanting more from him by remaining with him in their impoverished marriage (my interpretation).

The text (pg. 86 in Wordsworth Editions):

Mrs. Ramsey is knitting and picks up a book and reads at random a poem:

> "And all the lives we ever lived
> And all the lives we ever lived
> And all the lives to be,
> Are full of trees and changing leaves."

She felt she was climbing upwards and backwards and shoving up under petals that curved around her and only knew this is white or this is red... she turned the page, zigzagging this way and that... she heard her husband slapping his thighs... he seemed to be saying don't interrupt me... she went on sleeping... climbed up those branches laying hands on one flower after another

> "Not praise the deep vermillion in the rose"

How satisfying! How restful!... She awoke and was becoming conscious of her husband looking at her and thinking, *Go on reading...You don't look sad now*... and he exaggerated her simplicity for he liked to think she was not clever, not bookish, not learned at all... if she understood what she was reading.

Probably not (but)she was so beautiful... She took up her knitting and talked (Paul and Minta becoming engaged which she had encouraged). She thought, *why is it one wants people to marry? What is the value, the meaning of things?* **Every word they said would be true.** (My bold print and thoughts.) *There it is the truth, almost an aside; Do say something, she thought wishing only to hear his voice. The thing folding them in was beginning, she felt, to close round her again. Say anything, she begged, looking at him as if for help.*

"He was silent, swinging the compass on his watch and thinking of Balzac's and Scott's novels... coming together she could feel, coming side by side she could feel his mind like a raised hand... He said she wouldn't finish the stocving (she was knitting for the little boy) tonight. That's what she wanted—the asperity in his Voice reproving her. If he says it's wrong to be pessimistic probably it is wrong, she thought, the marriage will turn out all right." "No, she said, I shan't finish it."

As Part One closed, I felt deeply sad. He needs to lead the Charge to Do and Die; and to the victor goes the prize, everlasting fame, and a beautiful woman who can't say she loves him but needs his asperity. But she needs more. She needs to be valued not only for her beauty—which at age fifty is beginning to fade—as will the perfect table flowers fade and the perfect fruit bowl rot if left uneaten (a key dinner scene I leave for you to read); and to know their children who will not be young forever—the beautiful Pru he doesn't notice or the promising mathematician, Andrew, who needs love even if he doesn't win a scholarship (not that with eight kids to educate on an academic's income some money wouldn't be helpful—and as Mrs. R. keeps reminding herself and him the green house will cost 'fifty pounds,' a lot of money that they don't have to spare). And her needs for poetry, dreams and appreciation for her keen intellect, bookishness and generosity. Lilly Briscoe, the spinster who will never marry or have any children because she is not beautiful and will not allow men who might love her-Mr. Bankes or Mr. Tansey—because her picture isn't perfect—the tree isn't in the right place.

All of 'this mystery of the thing' exists as Woolf, the modernist, is making the case for new forms of art, poetry, novels, music, marriage, childrearing, politics—everything—while also eulogizing the dynamics and forms that live on and demand to be heard as well. The regularity of the sweep of the lighthouse beam is contrasted with the uncertainty of the weather and waves, life itself; and our unconscious minds, Freud and Horney with what Homer has to teach us about our unconscious drives, classical art and music with drip paintings and jazz; and war—always war—to be fought, not with charging horses and men with swords but with tanks and cannons and now women fighting alongside men flying helicopters and attack jets with missiles and cannons.

> "When can their glory fade?
> O the wild charge they made!
> All the world wondered.
> Honour the charge they made!
> Hour the Light Brigade,
> Noble six hundred!"

No, everything will not turn out all right.

VII.
Why read poetry and how to read poetry

My usual method of learning is to study texts—fiction or non-fiction, biographies or essays or textbooks, underline passages of interest to fix them in my mind even though I may never go back to them but know I always can look them up again; but the last paragraph of Zapruder's introduction (previously noted on page seven of this text)[8] resonated in my mind. He writes, "Most of all, I hoped when I was finished with this book, whenever anyone told me they don't know how to read poetry, I could hand them this book and say, I believe just by virtue of being alive you already do."

Of course, being alive isn't enough; curiosity, motivation, opportunity, having a community you want to reach, including yourself as a community of one—the side, conscious or barely conscious, your dream or daydream side, you want to reach—and perhaps most of all being open to introspection and having a comfort level with metaphor, symbols, art and music.

For example, when writing an essay as a pretend theatre critic, a story based on the myth of Orpheus and Eurydice, "I Would Follow You Anywhere, But Should I?" a Beatles song from their 1967 album *Sgt. Pepper's Lonely Hearts Club Band* came to mind, and I wrote, "Paul McCartney has something to say about this. Let's call him Orpheus and imagine he is singing to Eurydice—who has been

---

8   Zapruder, *Why Poetry,* Ibid.

disappointed by men and has turned down his proposal more than once. When she called him for help, he was so busy songwriting he couldn't hear her plea until it was too late, and so she knew deep down, she knew then and there that she couldn't trust him.[9]

"Will you still be sending me a valentine, birthday greeting, bottle of wine? If I'd been out to 'till quarter to four, would you lock the door? Will you still need me, will you still feed me when I'm sixty-four?"

I never was taught how to read poetry or to memorize poetry, and the popular straightforward rhymes with a message that resonates with me now that I am eighty-two are mostly love songs from my adolescence (Oscar Hammerstein, from *South Pacific, Wikipedia)*:

"Younger than springtime are you
Softer than starlight are you
Warmer than winds of June
Are the gentle lips you gave me
Gayer than
Laughter are you
Sweeter than music are you
Sunlight and moon beans
Heaven and earth
Are you to give me
And when your youth and joy
Invade my soul
And fill my heart…"

---

9   Schwartz, H. (2017). *Hide and Seek/Hidden and Found-In Search of a Balanced Life- Psychoanalytic Memoirs, Stories and Essays*. New York: IPBooks.

VIII.
Anita's poem of gratitude on her 80th birthday

Writing about love songs reminds me that I responded to my wife's best friend Anita on her 80th birthday, when she thanked her guests with a poem of gratitude by sending her a poem by a self-taught immigrant shopkeeper who wrote an ode to New Jersey and a Shakespeare sonnet in response to her plain-spoken poem of gratitude for her life entitled, "Lucky Me":

Lucky Me

A short while ago someone asked me what I would call a book if I were writing it about myself.
The thought that came to mind was, Lucky Me.

I spent the first ten years of my life in a home filled with love and happiness.
LUCKY ME.

My dad was warm and loving. Although he worked many hours and came home tired, we knew it was so that we could have the luxuries that we shared.

My mom kept a beautiful, immaculate home with the help of Clara, our housekeeper. Actually, she worked for us until she won a lottery, lots of money, and left to spend life with her pet Parrot.
Mom was the best mother and caregiver. I always felt that she should have been a nurse. She was by my side whenever needed.
LUCKY ME.

My younger brother was my best friend. We had so much fun together and genuinely loved each other. Of course, we did some nasty pranks in those first twelve years or so.
We kept each other's secrets, some major, some minor, and that has lasted throughout our lives. I also gained a wonderful sister-in-law.
LUCKY ME.

I chose to stay home for various reasons instead of going away to college. I attended Kean University and was there the first year that it opened. I had no problem living at home. Most of my friends came home after two years and we were together again as young adults. We had a fabulous circle of friends, many of whom are still in my life.
LUCKY ME.

I got married after my Junior year of college and finished school as a married woman. Many of my friends did the same. I taught school for one year, kindergarten. It was a great experience and I enjoyed the job. BUT then I got pregnant and started a kindergarten on my own.
Gabby and I had three children in less than five years. They were healthy and beautiful.
LUCKY ME.

In my thirties I became ill and was diagnosed with Aplastic Anemia, a deficiency of bone marrow, and spent nine months in Mt. Sinai Hospital, not a day went by when I did not have a visitor and support from more people than I could ever name. Some were platelet donors, some gave blood, all were loving and caring.
Here I am, almost 80, to tell you my story.
LUCKY ME.

Mom and Dad came home from Israel, where they had moved a few years before. They did a fabulous job along with my husband taking care of our children.
Before I came home my doctor told me that we would have to get rid of the dog, who was part of the family at that time or else I could not go home. I heard a story that the kids took a vote Mommy or Winnie (the dog), fortunately they voted for me.
LUCKY ME.

It is more than forty years later, there were some hard times but mostly a beautiful life, and I am here to say, LUCKY ME.

Today I am blessed with my children, Mitch and Emily, Kim and John and Jill and Scott.
They make me proud every day.

I have seven amazing grandchildren, Olivia, Max, Julia, Danielle, and Josh and Gabe.
And John.
LUCKY ME.

I would be remiss if I did not mention my friend, Susan, who has been like a sister to me for the past 70 years.

LUCKY ME.

I am so happy that you are all here to celebrate with me. Although I cannot believe the number, I accept it and know that my life has been blessed and I continue to say
LUCKY ME.

I also owe much of my happiness to Sandy, who has shared my life for almost eleven years.

My response to Anita:

Joseph Garlock
(1884–1980)
A Russian immigrant who left a legacy for New Jersey
and America
(Provenance provided by Steven Powers, painter and art dealer)

1959
"An Ode to New Jersey"

Age is a quality of mind
If you've left your dreams behind
If hope is cold
If you no longer look ahead
If your ambition fires are dead
Then you are old
But-if from life you take the best
In life you keep the zest
If love you hold

No matter how the years go by
No matter how the birthdays fly
You are not old.

A Sonnet for Anita

"Sonnet 18: Shall I Compare Thee to a Summer's Day?"
William Shakespeare

Shall I compare thee to a summer's day?
Thou art more lovely and more temperate:
Rough winds do shake the darling buds of May,
And summer's lease hath all too short a date;
Sometime too hot the eye of heaven shines,
And often is his gold complexion dimm'd;
And every fair from fair sometime declines,
By chance or nature's changing course untrimm'd;
But thy eternal summer shall not fade,
Nor lose possession of that fair thou ow'st;
Nor shall death brag thou wander'st in his shade,
When in eternal lines to time thou grow'st:
So long as men can breathe or eyes can see,
So long lives this, and this gives life to thee

IX.

Following Zapruder's suggestion to react to poetry that speaks to us in our time, I decided to read the poems in the weekly *New Yorker* first, rather than a movie review, gossip in the "The Talk of the Town," a short story, or an in-depth essay. As much of my concerns have been my mortality and a legacy, I want to leave something for my family and others who know me. I hit pay dirt on the my first try: Attribution: *The New Yorker,* December 9, 2009

The Green Lake
Dorothea Lasky

What work will you leave
I ask the Tailor
Who has sewn the button upon my shoe

Yesterday everything felt so hopeless
Now I have the energy to sit in the sun
All of the dammed seething baths
Now I am finally on my own

When I go places I call her
And unload my fashionable happenstance
I used to stop in the street and pick up an acorn
There were so many things I used to do

In the middle of the fire
I went and thought to mention it to the ghost
I have already burned, it said
His face was like my father's but was different

What work will you leave behind
I asked myself in the rain
Oh, this and that, it answered
And handed me the stars, then the moon

My associations to this mysterious poem:

The ghost answers me, gives me what I always wanted from my father, too much that he couldn't give; he is already burnedout, dead—but asks what legacy I want to leave. I minimize and he gives me everything he can—the universe—Motel the tailor in *Fiddler on the Roof* wishes for a sewing machine and names it a Singer—comforts with a button on a shoe, ah what a blessing to sore feet. Who is her? Mother, wife, daughter who cares about you regardless of your accomplishments. Regrets about the past, things I used to do; childhood pick up an acorn or kick a can or read a comic book? In the middle of the fire lives the ghost not any ghost, the Father and the son and the Holy Ghost the helper who has seen it all God the Creator—to create an idealized father, a transference persona His face was like my father's but was different—the magic of a father's love opens the world. But her mother accepts the chit chat of daily life and does not demand you to be fashionable. Is this mysterious poem a parable of the Holy Trinity and is the Green Lake a baptismal font?—strange associations by a Jewish writer who just happens to live next door to a Protestant Church which has a Manger each Christmas and across the street from a home with a huge spruce on their front lawn decorated with lovely white lights each year.

From a more prosaic point of view:

As I write I recall a talk given to our New Jersey Psychoanalytic Society by a very busy and accomplished senior analyst—not a scientific or clinical discussion, but a warning—make time for your family and pay attention to their comfort, their everyday needs. Ambition is fine, but what about a movie with your wife/husband or playing with your grandchildren. They are worth more than the stars and the moon.

X.
On Aging—Cicero

Cicero (106 BC–43 BC) was a Roman politician and lawyer who is considered one of Rome's greatest orators and prose stylists. *On Old Age* is an essay written on the subject of aging and death. It has remained popular because of its profound subject matter as well as its clear and beautiful language.

The treatise defends old age against its alleged disadvantages: "**First**, that it withdraws us from active pursuits; **second**, that it makes the body weaker; **third**, that it deprives us of almost all physical pleasures; and, **fourth**, that it is not far removed from death." He examines each claim in turn. **Cicero replies that older people remain active, just in different ways than their younger counterparts.** While they may be, according to the *Times Literary Supplement,* less physically adept, they may do more for their community, or they may be more introspective and philosophical. As he puts it: "Those... who allege that old age is devoid of useful activity... are like those who would say that the pilot does nothing in the sailing of his ship, because, while others are climbing the masts, or running about the gangways, or working at the pumps, he sits quietly in the stern and simply holds the tiller. He may not be doing what younger members of the crew are doing, but what he does is better and much more important. It is not by muscle, speed, or physical dexterity that great things are achieved, but by reflection, force of character, and judgment; in these qualities old age is usually not poorer but is even richer."

So, for Cicero, the prudence and wisdom that accompanies aging more than compensates for declining physical vigor. (Research has found that elders outperformed younger adults in understanding and solving complex social situations. [109]) He says that for Homer, Sophocles, Pythagoras, Plato, and others, old age did not "destroy their interests or take away their powers of expression." Old age can be a busy time where we continue lifelong projects or develop new interests.

I am now eighty-two and appreciate when a younger person, man or woman, offers me help to lift my carry-on luggage unto the overhead, or offers me a seat on the subway, or a stranger in the paint store offers to carry a bulky box of paint cans into the trunk of my car—while telling me about his spry one hundred-year-old grandmother—or my wife, who has better balance and understands my limitations, as do our daughters who warn both of us to be careful with stairs; and, last but not least, the sixteen-year-old who does yard work, puts up and takes down storm windows, changes light bulbs, and is now painting the basement concrete floor which I painted thirty years ago. Everyone calls me Sir, to which I jokingly respond, "Not necessary. I'm no longer in the Navy"—except in the South where everyone calls me Sir.

---

10 *Frontiers in Aging Neuroscience* 2015; 7: 120. Published online 2015 Jun 18

XI.
A poem from *The New Yorker*

While I have been reading poems in *The New Yorker* that I receive weekly, I will only include one more, a poem that frightened and puzzled me but forced me to respond to it:
The New Yorker-Jan 6, 2020

From the Catalogue of Cruelty
Donika Kelly

Once I slapped my sister with the back of my hand
We were so small, but I wanted to know

how it felt my hand raised high across
the opposite shoulder, slicing down like a trapeze
Her face caught in my hand. I'd slapped her in our
yellow room with the circus animal
on the curtains. I don't remember
how it felt. I was a rough child.

I said No. I said Those are my things.
I was speaking, usually of my socks:

white, athletic, thin and already gray
on the bottom, never where I left them.

I was speaking of my fists raining down
on my brother's back. My sister's socks.

In the fourth grade in California,
I kicked Charles in the testicles. At that school,

we played sock ball: hit the red playground ball
with the sides of our hands and ran the bases.
I kicked Charles with the top of my foot, caught him
In the hinge of ankle. I wanted to see

what would happen. I didn't believe
anything could hurt like it did on TV.

Charles folded in half at the crease of his waist.
My god, I was a rough child, but I believed

Charles, that my foot turned him into paper.
Later, I kicked my dad the same way,

but he did not crumple. It was summer
in Arkansas. What humidity
these children, full of water. I hit him
also, with the frying pan. I hit him

also, with the guitar. We laughed later:
Where had the guitar come from? My dad

was a star collapsing. The first thing
a dying star does is swell, swallow
whatever is near. He tried to take us
into his body, which was the house

the police entered. This how I knew
he was dying. I'd called the police.

What is your name? He tried to put us through
the walls of the house the police entered,

which was his body. What is your name?
Compromised: the integrity of a body

contracting. What is your name, sir? He answered:
Cronos. He answered: I'm hungry: He answered

A god long dead. He threw up all his children
right there on the carpet. After all,

we were so small, the children. The thing
about a star collapsing is that it knows

neither that it is a star nor in collapse.
Everything is stardust, everything is essential.

What is your name? Everything is resisting
arrest. Its gravity crushes the children

The officer didn't know the star's name

White dwarf? Black Hole? To see throw the collapsing star
face first into anything. Face first

into the back seat. Face first into the pepper
spray. Face first unto the precinct lawn.

Did you know you could throw a star? Do you
understand gravity, its weaknesses?
You are in my house. You should already know my name.

I was disturbed and puzzled by this poem—and hesitated to engage it—somehow it felt too close to home. But I had to. Who was Cronos and why should we care about him.[11]

Cronus was the King of the Titans and the god of time, in a particular time when he was viewed as a destructive, all-devouring force.

Ok, but this didn't help me much, because if Chronos is already named whose name should I know? ("You are in my house. You should already know my name.")

Then, like a bolt of lightning from Zeus, I knew the name was my own, my name.

As a boy I locked my brother, thirty-two months younger than me, in the basement to scare him—just because I could. He remembers it to this day and has not forgiven me. My mother believed I had caused his pectus excavatum (pigeon-breast), a benign anomaly of no medical significance, because I wanted to squeeze him to death, and that I had l pushed a little girl wading in a shallow ornamental pool with the intention of drowning her (no way). She never knew that one summer at a bungalow colony

---

11 https://www.theoi.com › Titan › Titan Krono

on a lakefront, I imagined a log to be a poisonous snake. How did I master that fear? By buying firecrackers and pinning non-poisonous garter snakes to the ground with a forked twig and blowing them up. And I was a good boy, non-violent and studious, but yet recognize myself in 'The Catalogue of Cruelty." As for my adolescence, I, at age seventeen, stole/borrowed our family car when my parents were out for the evening—probably visiting neighbors who lived within walking distance—determined to see if it would really go 100/mph on the nearby Garden State Parkway. It shook, rattled, and rolled; but went, just barely. All the while I expected a police car to pull me over, ask my name, throw me in the back of their cruiser, and take me to the precinct house to await my fate. As for eating children, loving parents say, "You're so sweet. I can eat you up," not thinking that their children might have nightmares of the big, bad wolf in grandma's clothing or Hansel and Gretel being thrown into an oven. Our parents are our stars, and sooner or later we need to accept their weaknesses, as inevitable as the pull of gravity.

XII.

As a collector of Japanese wood block prints from the Edo Period (1680-1867) it seems only fitting to introduce the Master of Haiku.

Basho
1644-1694

A Haiku to Basho
Maureen Nelson

Rooted as the tree
A smile spread from cheek to cheek
So peaceful and free

Brief Bio: (Dictionary.com)

Matsuo Basho (1644-1694), one of the greatest Japanese poets, elevated haiku to the level of serious poetry.... He was far from being an exponent of the new middle-class culture of the city dwellers of that day. Rather, in his poetry and in his attitude toward life, he seemed to harken back to a period some 300 years earlier. An innovator in poetry, spiritually and culturally, he maintained a great tradition of the past.

The haiku, a 17-syllable verse form divided into successive phrases or lines of 5, 7, and 5 syllables, originated in the linked verse of the 14th century, becoming an independent form in the latter part of the 16th century. Arakida Moritake (1473-1549) was a distinguished renga (linked poem) poet who originated witty and humorous verses he called haikai, which later became synonymous with haiku. Nishiyama Sōin (1605-1682), founder of the Danrin school, pursued Arakida's ideals. Basho was a member of this school at first, but breaking with it, he was responsible for elevating the haiku to a serious art, making it the verse form par excellence, which it has remained ever since.

In Kyoto ...
Basho
Translated by Jane Hirshfield

In Kyoto,
hearing the cuckoo,
I long for Kyoto.

Personal Note: The translation does not reflect the 5-7-5 form.

Excerpted from:
A History of Japanese Literature by William George Aston:

CHAPTER IV
POETRY OF THE SEVENTEENTH CENTURY—
HAIKAI, HAIBUN, KIŌKA

It would be absurd to put forward any serious claim on behalf of Haikai to an important position in literature. Yet, granted the form, it is difficult to see how more could be made of it than Basho has done. It is not only the meter which distinguishes these tiny effusions from prose. There is in them a perfection of apt phrase, which often enshrines minute but genuine pearls of true sentiment or pretty fancy. Specks even of wisdom and piety may sometimes be discerned upon close scrutiny. Suggestiveness is their most distinctive quality, as may be seen by the following:

"A cloud of flowers!
Is the bell Uyeno
Or Asakusa?"

To the English reader this will appear bald, and even meaningless. But to an inhabitant of Yedo, it conveys more than meets the ear. It carries him away to his favourite pleasure resort of Mukōjima, with its long lines of cherry-trees ranged by the bank of the river Sumida, and the difficulty in expanding it into something of this kind: "The cherry-flowers in Mukōjima are blossoming in such profusion as to form a cloud which shuts out the prospect. Whether the bell which is sounding from the distance is that of the temple of Uyeno or of Asakusa I am unable to determine."

A very large proportion of Bashō's Haikai are so obscurely allusive as to transcend the comprehension of the uninitiated foreigner. The following are some of the more lucid. The same quality of suggestiveness pervades them all.

"An ancient pond!
With a sound from the water
Of the frog as it plunges in."

"I come weary,
In search of an inn—
Ah! These wisteria flowers!"

"Ah! The waving lespedeza,
Which spills not a drop
Of the clear dew!"

"'Tis the first snow—
Just enough to bend
The gladiolus leaves!"

"Of Miïdera
The gate I would knock at—
The moon of to-day."

To the reader:

Haikus are hard to write. I thought of a dream I had some years ago. In five-seven-five meter:

"My computer awaits
A blank screen to write upon
Of love and lost youth"

Another Haiku more in the spirit of Basho:

The Arrival of Spring
Howard Schwartz

"Winter is so cold
Ah, red cardinals appear
On my patio"

A dialogue with Maureen Nelson who introduced me to Haiku:

In response to your Haiku,
I have written my own to you...

"Time knows no limit
As the past tells its story
　　　　　The heartstrings unfold"

Love it! OK, we are on a roll...

"Chaotic blood flow
Spills into my lover's heart
　　　　　Laughter gives us strength"

Something Roy (her new partner) and I do occasionally is: one of us would come up with a starting line of the Haiku, then the other would have to write the next... back and forth. We also would compose together. It is interesting to combine two mindsets to expand the lyrics.

Here's one for you if you wish to participate... And I think of you, and the conversation we once had about making footprints in the graveyard.

"Footprints lead the way.
How to recapture the past
When distance prevails"

And the last gift from Maureen in our dialogue

"Hear the children's cry
They grasp your heart and whisper
Sing a lullaby"

XIII.
A change of pace: *The Peanuts Papers*

Linus:
First appearance: September 19, 1952

"The benevolent, blanket-clutching philosopher always has a kind word for everybody... even his bossy older sister, Lucy. While he's often the voice of reason in the neighborhood, Linus also believes firmly in the Great Pumpkin, and he suffers more than most when people (or pumpkins) let him down. DID YOU KNOW: Linus wore glasses for a short time. Snoopy constantly stole them to torment him."
The Allen Ginsberg-Charles Schulz Mashup You Didn't Know You Needed[12]

---

12 *Electric Lit*: *Electric Literature* is a 501(c)(3) non-profit organization founded in 2009. Our mission is to amplify the power of storytelling with digital innovation, and to ensure that literature remains a vibrant presence in popular culture by supporting writers, embracing new technologies, and building community to broaden the audience for literature.

Grief (For Linus Van Pelt)" Part I
Jonathan Lethem

I saw the children of my neighborhood destroyed by mangle comics, disease comics, and gory comics, aggravating hysterical fussbudgets,
dragging themselves through the sarcastic streets at dawn looking for an angry plaid ice cream,
angelheaded blockheads obligated to play outside whenever the starry dynamo in the machinery of night is shining,
who spanking and roughnecked and hollow-eyed and high sat up smoking in the supernatural darkness of second childhoods floating across the tops of suburbs contemplating the chromatic fantasia,
who bared their brains to The Great Pumpkin under the El and saw goldfishes or horses or lambs or chipmunks staggering on suburban roofs illuminated, who passed through kindergarten with a piece of candy hidden in their ear hallucinating caramel and Beethoven among the scholars of income tax,
who were expelled from the nursery for crazy & publishing mud pies on the windowsills of the skull,
who cowered in toy rooms in diapers, leaving their candy bars on the sidewalk and listening to the test patterns through the wall,
who got busted in their sandboxes for putting their hand into a glass of milk, who hit one another with a piece of sod or drank lemonade in Paradise Alley, or hit their balls in the rough and were accused of killing snakes,
every winter it's the same thing, girls in stadium boots,

incomparable blind streets of shuddering cloud and lightning in
the mind leaping toward kite-eating trees, illuminating all the
motionless world of Time between,
humiliation of bare soup, backyard green tree cemetery dawns,
balloons supposed to be round, not square, storefront comic
racks of joyride soda fountain blinking traffic light, oh, you
dirty balloon, you better come back here, trash-can lid rantings,
the hustle and bustle of the city, to me there's nothing more
depressing than the sight of an empty old candy bag,
until the noise of wheels and children brought them down
shuddering mouth-wracked and battered bleak of brain all
drained of brilliance in the drear light of Zoo,
who sat there trying to make people think the wind is blowing,
a lost battalion of platonic tricyclists rolling along the curbs, whose
last pitches flew over
the backstop and rolled down the sewer,
yacketayakking screaming vomiting whispering facts and memories
and anecdotes and eyeball kicks and shocks of taxes, theology,
tadpoles, tamales, time-tables, tea and Tennessee Ernie,
who sat listening to the ocean roar, supposed be home taking a nap,
scared of a piece of fuzz on the sidewalk,
suffering Eastern sweats and bubble gum-chewings and migraines
of macaroni under candy-withdrawal on bleak curbs,
who drew a line clear around the world wondering where to go, and
went, leaving no broken hearts,
who just when you began to learn the technique your parents took
away your blanket,
who studied muskrat or mole? Mackerel? Or maybe mouse? Magna
charts? Mahler telepathy and bop kabbalah because the cosmos
instinctively vibrated at their feet,

who loned it through the streets here on earth among millions of people, while that tiny star was out there alone among millions of stars,

who thought they were only aggravating when thirty-three marshmallows gleamed in supernatural ecstasy,

who was doomed to go through life with nothing but a face

who lounged, all nervous and tense, with nothing more relaxing than to lie with your head in your water dish,

who put the girl in charge of the salt mines leaving behind nothing but the shadow of dungarees and the lava and ash of poetry,

whose poem is supposed to have feeling, whose poem couldn't touch anyone's heart, whose poem couldn't make anyone cry,

who gets depressed because he doesn't know how to turn the set on,

who while eating supper was fooling around and was told 'try to act like a human being' and replied "define human being,"

who broke down crying in white gymnasiums naked and trembling before the machinery of other skeletons,

who bit parents in the neck and shrieked with delight in cribs for committing no crime but their own wild cooking pederasty and intoxication,

who was a mess when he ate and a mess when he played and a mess when just standing still, but was at least consistent,

who let themselves be fucked in the ass by saintly motorcyclists, now what brought that on? Are you out of your mind? What are you trying to do, disgrace our family? Oh, the humiliation of it all, we'll probably have to move out of the neighborhood,

who went untouched and unmarred by modern civilization,

who hiccuped endlessly trying to giggle but wound up with a sob handing out lists of people's faults,

who without your blanket would crack like a piece of old bamboo, who is just about to starve to death when his grandma comes up with a baked-bean hot dish! The little kid wonders where the beans came from... then he notices something! His bean-bag is missing!

who if somebody likes you, he pats you on the head – if he doesn't like you, he kicks you,

who learned in medical circles the application of a spiritual tourniquet,

who wept at the romance of Halloween with their paper bags full of rocks and bad music, who said these rocks are especially groomed to be hurled in anger!

who sat in boxes breathing in the darkness, always felt sorry for amoebas, and in all the excitement forgot to feed the dog,

who wasn't sure whether he was going to end up in an orphanage or the humane society under the tubercular sky surrounded by orange crate racers of theology,

sometimes I think I'm a kind of vacant lot myself!

who scribbled all night rocking and rolling over lofty incantations which in the yellow morning were stanzas of gibberish, paypur, dore, howse, welkum, nice, spine!

awl this reeding is hard on mi eyes!

who cooked rotten animals lung heart feet tail dreaming of the pure vegetable kingdom, boy, I'm glad I'm not a lizard! I wonder if there are any dogs on the moon.

who plunged themselves under meat trucks looking for an egg, whose stomach has matured early, who last year was the only person you knew who had three hundred and sixty-five bad days, who threw their watches off the roof to "see time fly," & alarm clocks fell on their heads every day for the next decade,

in all the world there's nothing more inspiring that the sight of someone who has just been taken off the hook!

who shot him behind the Davenport this actually happened and if that isn't fatal, I don't know what is,
who had to erect some sort of mental fence to keep unpleasant news out of his mind,
and who therefore ran along the icy sidewalks obsessed with a sudden set of flashcards, only three years old and forced to go commercial,
who barreled down the sidewalks of the past journeying to each other's sandbox-Pigpen-solitude or first-leaf-to-die watch,
who tricycled seventy-two hours to find out if I had a vision or you had a vision, or he had a vision to just to find out insults seem to travel farther when the air is thin,
who nervous, lacking confidence, stupid and with poor taste and absolutely no sense of design,
yet the type of personality that will probably inspire a heroic symphony, a personality so simple that it defies analysis,
a fourteen-carat blockhead, a blockhead, a nitwit, a numbskull!
I'm only trying to give Charlie Brown a little destructive criticism!
Did you ever see a thief with such a round head?
I've been confused from the day I was born,
I have never pretended to be able to solve moral issues, I'm only human, I was an only dog, maybe I could blame it on society!
ah, Linus, while you are not safe, I am not safe, and now you're really in the total animal soup of time—
you're the only one who will follow me wherever I go!
if I were the only girl on earth, would you like me?
when you're a dog you don't have to worry like that... everything is clear cut, they're just imitation people,
I've never really seen an eclipse, that lemonade is full of weeds, what would you do if the moon fell right on your head?
can a person tear aside the veil of the future?

how about a pail of sand, old friend? to recreate the syntax of poor
   human prose and stand before you aggravating and doomed and
   shaking with shame,
putting down here what might be left to say in time come after
   death, the life you save may be a fussbudget,
and rising sort of tender-hearted, unable to bear to see the frightened
   faces of crazy salesmen,
with the absolute heart of the poem of life butchered out of their
   own bodies good to eat a thousand years,
the wrong person fell off that tricycle!

To read the rest of this poem and other work about *Peanuts*, check out *The Peanuts Papers: Charlie Brown, Snoopy & the Gang, and the Meaning of Life*: A Library of America Special Publication, October 22, 2019

XIV.

More poems from Maureen Nelson, the writer of Haikus, who has fallen in love again and rediscovered her eroticism. She has offered a personal statement:

When I returned to therapy after my husband died in 2012, I felt disembodied, and I had lost touch with my libidinal self. With time, as I moved through my grief, I allowed that part of myself along with my body as a whole, to return to life. Reconnecting with a long-lost love clearly awakened my sexuality and stimulated my desires and eroticism. This poem does speak to this awakening of desire, it is playful, lusty, and free, which is how I feel when I make love to my partner.

Unnamed
Maureen Nelson

Gather up my essence
Deep inside your blender
Lure me and stir me
Take me and shake me
Whip me and dip me
Blend me and bake me
Lick me and sip me
And then come back for more
To that place where I'll be waiting
Where time has no name
I'll be your protein milkshake
I'll be your healthy nosh
Like sweet and luscious candy

I'll be your honey baby
So, drink me till you're full___

The Man in the Moon
Maureen Nelson

Sometimes____
I feel illuminated
I could leap from crater
to crater
on the moon's surface____
Take rides through the
Night sky____
grab hold of the edge
of stars
and spin out of control__
This is how I feel
When you make love to me
Are you the man in the
Moon_____

XV.
An addendum to the Introduction

Sitting on the bookshelf behind my office desk was David Denby's *Lit Up*[13], only glanced at, but now of interest because I had read his *Great Books*, an account of his return to Columbia, our Alma Mater, to sit in on a class of freshmen to read the books they were reading—reading what he had read as a freshman and stimulating me to reread some of them too. In *LIT UP* he returns to the 10th grade classrooms of three schools—an inner city school in New Haven, a demanding upper West Side school in Manhattan, and a more affluent Westchester school serving Mamaroneck and Larchmont— where he "read all the stories, poems, plays, and novels that the students were reading along with their charismatic teacher, Mary Beth Jordan—and other 10th grade teachers- all with different approaches to teaching, but all with a determination to create readers with a lifelong interest and love of reading; classics and casual or so-called beach reading, and the ability to enjoy both. (Denby makes a judgement that only a prig reads only literary novels.).

I chose to focus on the Mamaroneck school because of its similarity to the high school in Newark, New Jersey, where I had great teachers, even though I have no recollection of being exposed to poetry, and Maplewood Middle School and Columbia High

---

13 David Denby, *Lit Up*, Henry Holt and Co, 2017.

School—where my wife was a guidance counselor at each of them for a year and told me stories of parents seeking reassignment of their children to the better teachers, the ones with a reputation for being more demanding. At Mamaroneck the 10th grade encouraged independent reading and compulsory reading and students read at least twenty-five books of their choosing during the school year. The teacher, in the classroom he sat in on, suggested books she had read or was reading and joined them as a fellow reader in their discussions. The school believed that immersion in reading was the best way to create readers from indifferent or non-readers, and that, "Part of the connection between classic texts and contemporary texts was that they intermingled in the reader's mind working on each other—usually in mysterious ways—to relate one book to another, the endless chain that made a reading life and that made a man and a woman too." (page 183)

Mary Beth Jordan
Mamaroneck High School, Tenth Grade: Reading list, page 240–241

> T.S. Eliot – "The Love Song of Alfred Prufrock"
> Theodore Roethke – "I Knew a Woman"
> Percy Bysshe Shelley – "To Wordsworth"
> Maxine Kumin – "Running Away Together"
> Robert Frost – "The Gift Outright"
> Woody Guthrie – "This Land is Your Land"
> Robert Frost – "Stopping by Woods on a Snowy Evening"
> & An Anecdote
> Robert Frost – "Christmas Trees a Circular Letter"

To the Reader:

With no further guidance from Ms. Jordan, I researched and made choices which spoke to me/moved me, reading several or more poems by each author. The poems I've chosen are in the public domain, often with scholarly discussions, but I have not consulted them, preferring to react to them in a personal way—as an adult student sitting in Beth Jordan's class, participating silently.

The Love Song of J. Alfred Prufrock
T.S. Eliot

Let us go then, you and I,
When the evening is spread out against the sky
Like a patient etherized upon a table;
Let us go, through certain half-deserted streets,
The muttering retreats
Of restless nights in one-night cheap hotels
And sawdust restaurants with oyster-shells:
Streets that follow like a tedious argument
Of insidious intent
To lead you to an overwhelming question...
Oh, do not ask, "What is it?"
Let us go and make our visit.
In the room the women come and go
Talking of Michelangelo.

The yellow fog that rubs its back upon the window-panes,
The yellow smoke that rubs its muzzle on the window-panes,
Licked its tongue into the corners of the evening,

Lingered upon the pools that stand in drains,
Let fall upon its back the soot that falls from chimneys,
Slipped by the terrace, made a sudden leap,
And seeing that it was a soft October night,
Curled once about the house, and fell asleep.

And indeed, there will be time
For the yellow smoke that slides along the street,
Rubbing its back upon the window-panes;
There will be time, there will be time
To prepare a face to meet the faces that you meet;
There will be time to murder and create,
And time for all the works and days of hands
That lift and drop a question on your plate;
Time for you and time for me,
And time yet for a hundred indecisions,
And for a hundred visions and revisions,
Before the taking of a toast and tea.

In the room the women come and go
Talking of Michelangelo.
And indeed, there will be time
To wonder, "Do I dare?" and, "Do I dare?"
Time to turn back and descend the stair,
With a bald spot in the middle of my hair—
(They will say: "How his hair is growing thin!")
My morning coat, my collar mounting firmly to the chin,
My necktie rich and modest, but asserted by a simple pin—
(They will say: "But how his arms and legs are thin!")
Do I dare
Disturb the universe?

HOWARD L. SCHWARTZ, M.D.

In a minute there is time
For decisions and revisions which a minute will reverse.

For I have known them all already, known them all:
Have known the evenings, mornings, afternoons,
I have measured out my life with coffee spoons;
I know the voices dying with a dying fall
Beneath the music from a farther room.
So how should I presume?

And I have known the eyes already, known them all—
The eyes that fix you in a formulated phrase,
And when I am formulated, sprawling on a pin,
When I am pinned and wriggling on the wall,
Then how should I begin
To spit out all the butt-ends of my days and ways?
And how should I presume?

And I have known the arms already, known them all—
Arms that are braceleted and white and bare
(But in the lamplight, downed with light brown hair!)
Is it perfume from a dress
That makes me so digress?
Arms that lie along a table or wrap about a shawl.
And should I then presume?
And how should I begin?

Shall I say, I have gone at dusk through narrow streets
And watched the smoke that rises from the pipes
Of lonely men in shirt-sleeves, leaning out of windows?...

I should have been a pair of ragged claws
Scuttling across the floors of silent seas.

And the afternoon, the evening, sleeps so peacefully!
Smoothed by long fingers,
Asleep ... tired ... or it malingers,
Stretched on the floor, here beside you and me.
Should I, after tea and cakes and ices,
Have the strength to force the moment to its crisis?
But though I have wept and fasted, wept and prayed,
Though I have seen my head (grown slightly bald) brought in upon a platter,
I am no prophet—and here's no great matter;
I have seen the moment of my greatness flicker,
And I have seen the eternal Footman hold my coat, and snicker,
And in short, I was afraid.

And would it have been worth it, after all,
After the cups, the marmalade, the tea,
Among the porcelain, among some talk of you and me,
Would it have been worthwhile,
To have bitten off the matter with a smile,
To have squeezed the universe into a ball
To roll it towards some overwhelming question,
To say: "I am Lazarus, come from the dead,
Come back to tell you all, I shall tell you all"—
If one, settling a pillow by her head
Should say: "That is not what I meant at all;
That is not it, at all."

And would it have been worth it, after all,

Would it have been worthwhile,
After the sunsets and the dooryards and the sprinkled streets,
After the novels, after the teacups, after the skirts that trail along the floor—
And this, and so much more?—
It is impossible to say just what I mean!
But as if a magic lantern threw the nerves in patterns on a screen:
Would it have been worth while
If one, settling a pillow or throwing off a shawl,
And turning toward the window, should say:
"That is not it at all,
That is not what I meant, at all."

No! I am not Prince Hamlet, nor was meant to be;
Am an attendant lord, one that will do
To swell a progress, start a scene or two,
Advise the prince; no doubt, an easy tool,
Deferential, glad to be of use,
Politic, cautious, and meticulous;
Full of high sentence, but a bit obtuse;
At times, indeed, almost ridiculous—
Almost, at times, the Fool.

I grow old... I grow old...
I shall wear the bottoms of my trousers rolled.

Shall I part my hair behind? Do I dare to eat a peach?
I shall wear white flannel trousers,
and walk upon the beach.
I have heard the mermaids singing, each to each.

I do not think that they will sing to me.

I have seen them riding seaward on the waves
Combing the white hair of the waves blown back
When the wind blows the water white and black.
We have lingered in the chambers of the sea
By sea-girls wreathed with seaweed red and brown
Till human voices wake us, and we drown.

Yes, I too am aging and as I grow old this poem speaks to my need to accept the inevitable end that will come to us all. It is a telling love song to life I hear as I read or sing it out loud, an elegy to the tastes and sounds of life—our healthy narcissism to sustain us until the end. (Bold print mine).

I grow old ... I grow old ...
I shall wear the bottoms of my trousers rolled.
Shall I part my hair behind? Do I dare to eat a peach?
I shall wear white flannel trousers,
and walk upon the beach.
I have heard the mermaids singing, each to each.
I do not think that they will sing to me.

I have seen them riding seaward on the waves
Combing the white hair of the waves blown back
When the wind blows the water white and black.
We have lingered in the chambers of the sea
By sea-girls wreathed with seaweed red and brown
Till human voices wake us, and we drown

Songs consecrated to truth and liberty

It seems I, age eighty-two, am choosing poems about lost childhood and youth and friends—mourning the lost sweet young love, that departs which never may return...childhood and youth, friendship and love's first glow, have fled like sweet dreams, leaving thee (me) to mourn.
I have felt this too. But would a 10th grade class choose these poems? Perhaps? They have lost friends who moved away, teachers who have died, parents who have died early of illness or in war, or as a result of a bitter divorce—the children shuttling from one bedroom to another—or grandparents or their homeland as refugees, perhaps not in Mamaroneck, but through empathic identification with those children they see in the news on their cell phones—washed ashore dead in the arms of a desperate father or at sea in over-crowded rafts. This might be a poem best read to them by one of those gifted teachers who participates in the program of voluntary reading by telling them which Shelley poem she voluntarily chose and why she did.

Ah, but Roethke speaks to me:

I Knew a Woman
Theodore Roethke

I knew a woman lovely in her bones,
When small birds sighed, she would sigh back at them;
Ah, when she moved, she moved more ways than one:
The shapes a bright container can contain!
Of her choice virtues only gods should speak,

Or English poets who grew up on Greek
(I'd have them sing in chorus, cheek to cheek).

Love likes a gander, and adores a goose:
Her full lips pursed, the errant note to seize;
She played it quick, she played it light and loose;
My eyes, they dazzled at her flowing knees;
Her several parts could keep a pure repose,
Or one hip quiver with a mobile nose
(She moved in circles, and those circles moved).

Let seed be grass, and grass turn into hay:
I'm martyr to a motion not my own;
What's freedom for? To know eternity.
I swear she cast a shadow white as stone.
But who would count eternity in days?
These old bones live to learn her wanton ways:
(I measure time by how a body sways)."

Running Away Together
Maxine Kumin

It will be an island on strings
well out to sea and austere
bobbing as if at anchor
green with enormous fir trees
formal as telephone poles.

We will arrive there slowly
hand over hand without oars.

Last out, you will snip the fragile
umbilicus white as a beansprout
that sewed us into our diaries.

We will be two bleached hermits
at home in our patches and tears.
We will butter the sun with our wisdom.
Our days will be grapes on a trellis
perfectly oval and furred.

At night we will set our poems
adrift in ginger ale bottles
each with a clamshell rudder
each with a piggyback spider
waving them off by dogstar

and nothing will come from the mainland
to tell us who cares, who cares
and nothing will come of our lovelock
except as our two hearts go soft
and black as avocado pears.

It will be an island on strings
well out to sea and austere
bobbing as if at anchor
green with enormous fir trees
formal as telephone poles.

We will arrive there slowly
hand over hand without oars.

Last out, you will snip the fragile
umbilicus white as a beansprout
that sewed us into our diaries.

We will be two bleached hermits
at home in our patches and tears.
We will butter the sun with our wisdom.
Our days will be grapes on a trellis
perfectly oval and furred.

At night we will set our poems
adrift in ginger ale bottles
each with a clamshell rudder
each with a piggyback spider
waving them off by dogstar

and nothing will come from the mainland
to tell us who cares, who cares
and nothing will come of our lovelock
except as our two hearts go soft
and black as avocado pears.

Every kid will get this, especially those who have already read *Robinson Crusoe* or Mark Twain or seen the movie *Castaway*. Summarized by a reviewer on the site <u>Plugged'n:</u>

"Chuck Noland is a FedEx system's engineer whose personal and professional life are ruled by the clock. His fast-paced career takes him, often at a moment's notice, to far-flung locales and away from his girlfriend, Kelly. On one such trip, Chuck's manic existence abruptly halts when his plane goes down in the middle of the Pacific Ocean and he becomes stranded on a remote, uninhabited island. He is the only survivor... Chuck makes the best of it. First, he must find a way to meet basic human needs (food, water and shelter), which he accomplishes with the help of various FedEx packages that have washed ashore with him...

Once Chuck's physical needs are met, his biggest struggle involves his emotional and psychological health. He must resist desperation and not reach the point of cracking up. Daniel Defoe's 18th Century literary hero, *Robinson Crusoe*, turned to a Bible and found God in the midst of nothingness. Chuck Noland befriends a volleyball. Fate finally offers Chuck a chance to escape the island on a raft. After a heroic struggle, he is saved and brought home. It's an ironic twist that Chuck's problem-solving background helps him survive being a castaway while the skills learned as a castaway help him adapt to a new life in civilization."

> At night we will set our poems
> adrift in ginger ale bottles
> each with a clamshell rudder
> each with a piggyback spider
> waving them off by dogstar

Chuck survives and delivers his packages—better late than never.

Another digression to introduce Maxine Kumin and thank Beth Jordan who put her on her 10th grade poetry syllabus. There's no room in this book to choose more than two poems, but there is room on my bookshelves to buy more of her books of poetry.

Introduction to Maxine Kumin: Wikipedia

An enduring presence in American poetry, Maxine Kumin's career spanned over half a century. Maxine Kumin (née Winokur) was born to a Reform Jewish family in Germantown, Pennsylvania. She attended Catholic and public schools before earning a BA and MA from Radcliffe College and married Victor Kumin in 1946 while still a student, and she would have two daughters and a son. On her early writing days, Kumin remarked, "began writing poetry in the Dark Ages of the '50s with very little sense of who I was—a wife, a daughter, a mother, a college instructor, a swimmer, a horse lover, a hermit." She was the recipient of prestigious awards such as the Pulitzer Prize, the Ruth Lilly Poetry Prize, and an American Academy and Institute of Arts and Letters Award. She was the poetry consultant for the Library of Congress (now known as the US poet laureate position) in 1981-1982, and taught at many of the country's most prestigious universities, including MIT, Princeton University, and Columbia University.

From Maxine Kumin *Selected Poems-1960 1990—New York Times*, a Notable Book of the Year, W.W. Norton (1997), New York—two poems that moved me, not about nature, farm life and horses (I'm a city kid who graduated Columbia College'59 and grew up in a mostly Jewish section of Newark, New Jersey), but a poem about the Holocaust and a poem she wrote at age 82 to her first love, Victor Kumin, a Harvard boy she met in 1946, when she was 21 years old, shortly after their first date. (These poems are on public domain web sites.)

HOWARD L. SCHWARTZ, M.D.

Looking Back in My Eighty-First Year
Maxine Kumin

How did we get to be old ladies my
grandmother's job—when we
were the long-legged girls?
— Hilma Wolitzer

Instead of marrying the day after graduation,
in spite of freezing on my father's arm as
here comes the bride struck up,
saying, I'm not sure I want to do this,

I should have taken that fellowship
to the University of Grenoble to examine
the original manuscript
of Stendhal's unfinished Lucien Leeuwen,

I, who had never been west of the Mississippi,
should have crossed the ocean
in third class on the Cunard White Star,
the war just over, the Second World War

when Kilroy was here, that innocent graffito,
two eyes and a nose draped over
a fence line. How could I go?
Passion had locked us together.

Sixty years my lover,
he says he would have waited.

He says he would have sat
where the steamship docked

till the last of the pursers
decamped, and I rushed back
littering the runway with carbon paper...
Why didn't I go? It was fated.

Marriage dizzied us. Hand over hand,
flesh against flesh for the final haul,
we tugged our lifeline through limestone and sand,
lover and long-legged girl.

In the Absence of Bliss
Maxine Kumin

Museum of the Diaspora, Tel Aviv
The roasting alive of rabbis
in the ardor of the Crusades
went unremarked in Europe from
the Holy Roman Empire to 1918,
open without prerequisite
when I was an undergraduate.

While reciting the Sh'ma in full
expectation that their souls
would waft up to the bosom
of the Almighty the rabbis burned,
pious past the humming extremes
of pain. And their loved ones with them.

Whole communities tortured and set aflame
in Christ's name
while chanting Hear, O Israel.

Why?
Why couldn't the rabbis recant,
kiss the Cross, pretend?
Is God so simple that He can't
sort out real from sham?
Did He want
these fanatic autos-da-fé, admire
the eyeballs popping,
the corpses shrinking in the fire?

We live in an orderly
universe of discoverable laws,
writes an intelligent alumna
in Harvard Magazine.
Bliss is belief,
agnostics always say
a little condescendingly
as befits mandarins who function
on a higher moral plane
Consider our contemporary
Muslim kamikazes
hurling their explosives-
packed trucks through barriers.
Isn't it all the same?
They too die cherishing the fond
certitude of a better life beyond.

We walk away from twenty-two
graphic centuries of kill-the-Jew
and hail, of all things, a Mercedes
taxi. The driver is Yemeni,
loves rock music and hangs
each son's picture—three so far—
on tassels from his rearview mirror.

I do not tell him that in Yemen
Jewish men, like women, were forbidden
to ride their donkeys astride,
having just seen this humiliation
illustrated on the Museum screen.

When his parents came
to the Promised Land, they entered
the belly of an enormous
silver bird, not knowing whether
they would live or die.
No matter. As it was written,
the Messiah had drawn nigh.
I do not ask, who tied
the leaping ram inside the thicket?
Who polished, then blighted the apple?
Who loosed pigs in the Temple,
set tribe against tribe
and nailed man in His pocket?

But ask myself, what would
I die for and reciting what?

Not for Yahweh, Allah, Christ,
those patriarchal fists
in the face. But would
I die to save a child?
Rescue my lover? Would
I run into the fiery barn
to release animals,
singed and panicked, from their stalls?

Bliss is belief, but where's
the higher moral plane I roost on?
This narrow plank given to splinters.
No answers. Only questions.
Museum of the Diaspora, Tel Aviv
The roasting alive of rabbis
in the ardor of the Crusades
went unremarked in Europe from
the Holy Roman Empire to 1918,
open without prerequisite
when I was an undergraduate.

While reciting the Sh'ma in full
expectation that their souls
would waft up to the bosom
of the Almighty the rabbis burned,
pious past the humming extremes
of pain. And their loved ones with them.
Whole communities tortured and set aflame
in Christ's name
while chanting Hear, O Israel.

Why?
Why couldn't the rabbis recant,
kiss the Cross, pretend?
Is God so simple that He can't
sort out real from sham?
Did He want
these fanatic autos-da-fé, admire
the eyeballs popping,
the corpses shrinking in the fire?

We live in an orderly
universe of discoverable laws,
writes an intelligent alumna
in Harvard Magazine.
Bliss is belief,
agnostics always say
a little condescendingly
as befits mandarins who function
on a higher moral plane.

Consider our contemporary
Muslim kamikazes
hurling their explosives-
packed trucks through barriers.
Isn't it all the same?
They too die cherishing the fond
certitude of a better life beyond.

We walk away from twenty-two
graphic centuries of kill-the-Jew
and hail, of all things, a Mercedes

taxi. The driver is Yemeni,
loves rock music and hangs
each son's picture—three so far—
on tassels from his rearview mirror.

I do not tell him that in Yemen
Jewish men, like women, were forbidden
to ride their donkeys astride,
having just seen this humiliation
illustrated on the Museum screen.

When his parents came
to the Promised Land, they entered
the belly of an enormous
silver bird, not knowing whether
they would live or die.
No matter. As it was written,
the Messiah had drawn nigh.

I do not ask, who tied
the leaping ram inside the thicket?
Who polished, then blighted the apple?
Who loosed pigs in the Temple,
set tribe against tribe
and nailed man in His pocket?

But ask myself, what would
I die for and reciting what?
Not for Yahweh, Allah, Christ,
those patriarchal fists
in the face. But would

I die to save a child?
Rescue my lover? Would
I run into the fiery barn
to release animals,
singed and panicked, from their stalls?

Bliss is belief, but where's
the higher moral plane I roost on?
This narrow plank given to splinters.
No answers. Only questions.

Back to Ms. Jordan's suggested reading list:

The Gift Outright
Robert Frost
Poem recited at John F. Kennedy's Inauguration

The land was ours before we were the land's
She was our land more than a hundred years
Before we were her people. She was ours
In Massachusetts, in Virginia,
But we were England's, still colonials,
Possessing what we still were unpossessed by,
Possessed by what we now no more possessed.
Something we were withholding made us weak
Until we found out that it was ourselves
We were withholding from our land of living,
And forthwith found salvation in surrender.
Such as we were, we gave ourselves outright
(The deed of gift was many deeds of war)

To the land vaguely realizing westward,
But still unstoried, artless, unenhanced,
Such as she was, such as she will become.

Another poem as a response to "The Gift Outright"

This Land Is Your Land
Woody Guthrie

This Land Is Your Land
This land is my land
From California to the New York island
From the Redwood Forest, to the gulf stream waters
This land was made for you and me
As I went walking that ribbon of highway
I saw above me that endless skyway
And saw below me that golden valley
This land was made for you and me
I roamed and rambled, and I followed my footsteps
To the sparkling sands of her diamond deserts
And all around me, a voice was sounding
This land was made for you and me
When the sun comes shining, then I was strolling
In the wheat fields waving and dust clouds rolling
The voice was chanting as the fog was lifting
This land was made for you and me
This land is your land and this land is my land

Robert Frost, when asked what his favorite poem was, said:

Stopping by Woods on a Snowy Evening
Robert Frost

Whose woods these are I think I know.
His house is in the village though;
He will not see me stopping here
To watch his woods, fill up with snow.

My little horse must think it queer
To stop without a farmhouse near
Between the woods and frozen lake
The darkest evening of the year.

He gives his harness bells a shake
To ask if there is some mistake.
The only other sound's the sweep
Of easy wind and downy flake.

The woods are lovely, dark and deep,
But I have promises to keep,
And miles to go before I sleep,
And miles to go before I sleep.

Also:

Library of America Article in their Story of the Week

"Christmas Trees"
Robert Frost (1874–1963)

From *Robert Frost: Collected Poems, Prose, & Plays* (Library of America, 1995)

In 1947 a student from the University of Maine, N. Arthur Bleau, attended a lecture Robert Frost gave at Bowdoin College. During the Q&A session, Bleau asked Frost to name his favorite poem, and the poet declined to answer. But afterward Frost spoke to the young man privately and said, "I'd have to say, "Stopping by the Woods on a Snowy Evening" is that poem." Frost then related an anecdote, which Bleau records in an essay thirty years later.

In one of the early years of the century, three days before Christmas on the night of the equinox—in the poem, "The darkest evening of the year"—Frost hitched up his horse to the sleigh and, with a snowstorm on the horizon, journeyed two miles to Derry Village, New Hampshire, to sell some farm produce so he could buy Christmas presents for the children. Unable to sell anything, he returned home. "It had started to snow, and his heart grew heavier with each step of the horse.

Around the next bend in the road, near the woods, they would come into view of the house. He knew the family was anxiously awaiting him. How could he face them? What could he possibly say or do to spare them the disappointment he felt?

They entered the sweep of the bend. The horse slowed down and then stopped. It knew what he had to do. He had to cry, and he did. I recall the very words he spoke. "I just sat there and bawled like a baby"—until there were no more tears.

In a postscript to the essay, Frost's daughter Lesley confirmed the story, which her father had told her separately, also during the 1940s, almost "word for word" as it was told to Bleau.

Also, of interest is the letter he wrote on Christmas 1916:

"Christmas Trees"
A Christmas Circular Letter

Originally published in *Mountain Interval* (1916)

The city had withdrawn into itself
And left at last the country to the country;
When between whirls of snow not come to lie
And whirls of foliage not yet laid, there drove
A stranger to our yard, who looked the city,
Yet did in country fashion in that there
He sat and waited till he drew us out
A-buttoning coats to ask him who he was.
He proved to be the city come again
To look for something it had left behind
And could not do without and keep its Christmas.
He asked if I would sell my Christmas trees;
My woods—the young fir balsams like a place
Where houses all are churches and have spires.
I hadn't thought of them as Christmas trees.
I doubt if I was tempted for a moment
To sell them off their feet to go in cars
And leave the slope behind the house all bare,
Where the sun shines now no warmer than the moon.
I'd hate to have them know it if I was.
Yet more I'd hate to hold my trees except
As others hold theirs or refuse for them,
Beyond the time of profitable growth,
The trial by market everything must come to.
I dallied so much with the thought of selling.
Then whether from mistaken courtesy

And fear of seeming short of speech, or whether
From hope of hearing good of what was mine,
I said, 'There aren't enough to be worthwhile.'

'I could soon tell how many they would cut,
You let me look them over.'

'You could look.
But don't expect I'm going to let you have them.'
Pasture they spring in, some in clumps too close
That lop each other of boughs, but not a few
Quite solitary and having equal boughs
All round and round. The latter he nodded 'Yes' to,
Or paused to say beneath some lovelier one,
With a buyer's moderation, 'That would do.'
I thought so too but wasn't there to say so.
We climbed the pasture on the south, crossed over,
And came down on the north.

He said, "A thousand.'
'A thousand Christmas trees!—at what apiece?"

He felt some need of softening that to me:
'A thousand trees would come to thirty dollars.'

Then I was certain I had never meant
To let him have them. Never show surprise!
But thirty dollars seemed so small beside
The extent of pasture I should strip, three cents
(For that was all they figured out apiece),
Three cents so small beside the dollar friends

I should be writing to within the hour
Would pay in cities for good trees like those,
Regular vestry-trees whole Sunday Schools
Could hang enough on to pick off enough.
A thousand Christmas trees I didn't know I had!
Worth three cents more to give away than sell,
As may be shown by a simple calculation.
Too bad I couldn't lay one in a letter.
I can't help wishing I could send you one
In wishing you herewith a Merry Christmas.

XVI.

Not on the 10th grade reading list at Mamaroneck but in the spirit of students bringing to class poems they had read on their own, here's mine:

To Bruce Springsteen

To a Jersey guy—like me—and to my vacations in Bradley Beach, Belmar, and Asbury Park where the Stone Pony, right off the Boardwalk, "launchpad for many American music legends, including New Jersey natives Bruce Springsteen, Jon Bon Jovi, and Southside Johnny and the Asbury Jukes." (Wikipedia)
Springsteen's lyrics are gritty prose poems that speak to the need to escape the bounds of New Jersey, take risks and find love—as I did at age eighteen with the girl I married at age twenty-three. We dated "down the shore," necked under the boardwalk, then a movie, and cheap Chinese dinner before the drive home, traveling not by motorcycle but in a car I bought for 100 bucks. I graduated from Weequahic High School, Newark, New Jersey in 1955.

Suggestion: Listen to the You Tube Video

Born to Run
Bruce Springsteen

In the day we sweat it out on the streets
Of a runaway American dream
At night we ride through the mansions of glory
In suicide machines
Sprung from cages on Highway 9
Chrome wheeled, fuel injected, and steppin' out over the line
Oh, baby this town rips the bones from your back
It's a death trap, it's a suicide rap
We gotta get out while we're young
'Cause tramps like us, baby, we were born to run
Yes, girl, we were
Wendy, let me in, I wanna be your friend
I wanna guard your dreams and visions
Just wrap your legs 'round these velvet rims
And strap your hands 'cross my engines
Together we could break this trap
We'll run 'til we drop, baby, we'll never go back
Oh, will you walk with me out on the wire?
'Cause, baby, I'm just a scared and lonely rider
But I gotta know how it feels
I want to know if love is wild

Then a surprise poem appears—not by reindeer or under a tree— but by an opinion writer for the *New York Times* commenting on the impeachment hearings of President Trump going on as I was working on this book:

A Poem on the Eve of Impeachment
Frank Bruni
(*New York Times*, Dec. 18, 2019)

The articles were drafted by Democrats with care
In hopes that a conscience would soon bloom there.

We pundits were tossing all steamed in our beds,
While Trump's certain acquittal danced in our heads.

And I in frustration, feeling all solemn,
Wished I could capture my woe in a column,

When out on the web there arose such a clatter,
I signed into Twitter to see what was the matter.

And there I beheld him, the master of lies,
Weaving fresh falsehoods, to no one's surprise.

He savaged the Bidens, he smeared Adam Schiff,
And cycled through villains in a furious jiff,

Not to mention distractions, like the teeth of the Speaker.
Could a "leader" be cruder, could his morals be weaker?

So now he's a dentist, in his all-knowing ways?
I prayed for deliverance one of these days.

When what to my cynical eyes did appear
But a raft of excuses pulled by mangy reindeer,

With a weasel-eyed driver, so meek and so zany,
I knew in a moment he must be Mulvaney.

More shameless than con men, the sycophants came,
And Trump gloated, so bloated, and called them by name:

"Now, Rudy! Now, Jared! Now, Lindsey and Mitch!
Please fly this democracy into a ditch!

It is how you will save me. It is how I prevail.
Or else I will join poor Paul in the jail.

That's the toll of a presidency ended too soon,
So, you must sing along to my favorite tune:

'It's a witch hunt! A hoax!' Those are lyrics for me.
That's the verse, that's the chorus, for eternity."

He was dressed in a necktie, from his jowls to his soles.

His hair, how it swirled! His legs, how they splayed!
On such fishy foundations was his confidence laid.

And we couldn't stop looking—not his fans, not his foes.
That was what he was after: the show of all shows.

Its plot strained belief. Its appeal tested reason.
Still it was soaring toward a second season.

The economy roared. The Democrats whimpered.
Vladimir chortled. Emmanuel simpered.

In the bag that Trump carried, he had goodies galore:
Lower taxes, the Dow, right-wing judges and more.

They weren't for the many, they favored the few,
But that was obscured by the smoke that he blew.

All was fog, all was mist, all was boast, all was fiction,
As he hid his true airs with bad diet and diction.

He could do as he wanted and never know fear,
For an elf—and a savior!—named Barr hovered near.

And then there was Tucker and of course Hannity
To put an extra-fine gloss on insanity.

What great luck to discover a country so riven
You could smash it and rule it if suitably driven.

You could summon the Russians, you could bully Ukraine,
Just as long as you made "It's fake news!" your refrain.

I cringed as I watched him and cried for us all,
Our values, our futures hijacked by his gall.

A last bid to preserve them was caused to impeach
But his party's corruption put him beyond reach.

So then why all his thrashing? His howls of dejection?
It was just a performance for the next election.

It brought more donations. It rallied the base.
You could see, if you looked, a clear smirk on his face.

If you listened, you heard it: a lilt in his voice.
In drama like this, he would always rejoice.

So, as history scarred him, he could nonetheless yell,
"Merry TrumpMas to all! I'm the king of this hell."

My comment on Bruni's poem:

Matthew Zapruder in *Why Poetry*[14] writes, "The usefulness of poetry has less to do with delivering a message (which we can just easily get from prose), and far more to do with what poems can easily do to our language, reinventing it and reactivating it, and thereby drawing us into a different form of attention and awareness.

---

14 Ibid, Zapruder, *Why Poetry*.

XVII.

While finding that poetry is everywhere once I had eyes to see it, the Library of America (see previous contributions from LOA, to which I subscribe) announced their publication of *The Mark Twain Anthology—Great Writers on His Life and Work*[15] (H.L. Mencken, Toni Morrison, Helen Keller, Ernest Hemingway, T.S. Eliot—on and on.) What follows are several of the many that I particularly liked that reveal Twain the poet, or were referred to him by another poet, or are unique poems about him written by a poet.

Helen Keller writes of a visit with her dear friend Samuel Clemens who said that he was very lonely and told her that when guests "have departed my thoughts trail away into the past. I think of Susy (his daughter who died of spinal meningitis at age 24), and my wife Livy, and I seem to fumble in the dark folds of confused dreams. I come upon memories of little intimate happenings of long ago that drop like stars into the silence. One day everything breaks and crumbles. It did the day Livy died." Mr. Clemens repeated with emotion and inexpressible tenderness the lines he had carved on Susy's headstone:

---

15 Mark Twain, *The Mark Twain Anthology—Great Writers on His Life and Work*, Library of America Literary Classics, New York, 2019.

Warm Summer Sun
Mark Twain

Warm summer sun,
Shine kindly here,
Warm southern wind,
Blow softly here.
Green sod above,
Lie light, lie light.
Good night, dear heart,
Good night, good night.

Mark Twain's daughter Olivia Susan Clemens died on August 18, 1896 at the age of twenty-four. She was buried in the Clemens family plot at Woodlawn Cemetery in Elmira, New York. A frequent question that arises is related to the poem that her father had placed upon her headstone.

The lines were adapted from a poem titled "Annette" written by writer Robert Richardson, sometimes identified as a native of Australia. The poem was published in a book titled *Willow and Wattle* (1893). The original poem in its entirety reads:

Annette
Robert Richardson

And they say, Annette, that you
Broke a foolish heart or two;
Can, I wonder, this be true?
Yet I will admit, Annette,
That you were a sad coquette;

Fain of praise and fain of kisses,
Fond of all the farthing blisses
That for fallen man unmeet are,
So they tell us, yet so sweet are
Fond of your glad world, and this is
All the blame I can recall
That on your young head should fall -
And I knew you best of all.
Save thought and little care
Than to braid your rippled hair,
Ribbon blue or crimson wear
Who in all this giddy fair
Who so bright and debonair?
Yet me thought, Annette, you were
just a little tired sometimes
Hearing of the midnight chimes
Weary of the passing show,
Tired of rout, and Park, and Row;
Longing for the night's retreat,—
Weary little heart and feet.
Dancing days are quickly run—
Dead, and only twenty-one!
Ne'er so glad as when you had
Twenty lovers, man and lad,
Round you waiting for a glance
From your radiant beaux yeux
(Certes, they were very blue).
Twenty lovers in a row
Callow gallants, faded beaux,
I have seen them come and go,
Waiting patient for the chance

Of a single fleeting dance;
Mayfair's youth and chivalry
Bent to you their courtly knee.
Never more shall feet of yours
Lightly lead the laughing hours,
Lead the waltz's dreamy dance
To the " fair old tunes of France."
Dancing days are fleetly run—
Dead, and only twenty-one!
If that ancient ethic view
Of Pythagoras be true,
Your light soul is surely now
In that bird upon the bough,
Singing, with soft-swelling throat,
To the wind that heeds it not;
Or in that blue butterfly,
Flitting like a jewel by,
Flashing golden to the sun.
Soon, like yours, its day is run—
Dead, and only twenty-one!
Dead a week, and not already
Quite forgotten--nay, what right have
I to doubt it; sure, we might have
Easier missed a wiser lady.
Over you the grass will blow,
Springs will come, and autumns go.
Will you, Annette, ever know
There remain here one or two
Who will still remember you?—
O'er whose memory, now and then,
With a thought of sad, sweet pain,

There will cross your fair flower face,
And the bright coquettish grace,
With the memory of old days.
Somewhere there beyond the blue,
In the mansions that so many
Are, they say, is there not any
One of all, Annette, for you?
You, whose only trespass this is
That you loved the farthing blisses,
Broke a foolish heart in twain
That would lightly mend again.
Warm summer sunshine friendly here
Warm western wind, blow kindly here;
Green sod above, rest light, rest light,
Good-night, Annette!
Sweetheart, good-night!

Albert Bigelow Paine, in his biography of Mark Twain, notes that over the years the lines on Susy's headstone were generally attributed to Twain himself. When this was reported to him, he ordered the name of the poet Robert Richardson to be cut into the stone beneath them.

On January 22, 1907, when Twain was dictating portions of his autobiography, he recalled that he had forgotten the name of the author of the poem: "We had found them in a book in India but had lost the book and with it the author's name. But in time an application to the editor of 'Notes and Queries' furnished me the author's name... and it has been added to the verse upon the gravestone."

The last stanza of Richardson's poem is Susy's epitaph:

Warm summer sunshine friendly here
Warm western wind, blow kindly here;
Green sod above, rest light, rest light,
Good-night, Annette!
Sweetheart, good-night.

Edward Field (Wikipedia Bio): born 1924, a poet, novelist and memoirist, was born in Brooklyn and lived in Greenwich Village most of the last half century... whose "quirky, impassioned and often political poems have been likened to works by Allen Ginsburg and Walt Whitman...has brought his Jewish heritage into a number of his poems. The cadence of the imaginary conversation that takes place in this poem between Twain and Aleichem reflect the cadences of Yiddish that floated through Field's Brooklyn childhood." (LOA: *The Mark Twain Anthology*)

Mark Twain and Sholom Aleichem
Edward Field

Mark Twain and Sholom Aleichem went one day to Coney Island—
Mark wearing a prison-striped bathing costume and straw hat,
Sholom in greenish-black suit, starched collar, beard,
Steel-rimmed schoolmaster glasses, the whole works,
And an umbrella that he flourished like an actor,
Using it sometimes to hurry along the cows

As he described scenes of childhood in the village in Poland,
Or to spear a Jew on a sword like a cossack.

Sitting together on the sand among food wrappers and lost coins,
They went through that famous dialogue
Like the vaudeville routine After-you-Gaston:
"They tell me you are called the Yiddish Mark Twain."

"Nu? The way I heard it; you are the American Sholom Aleichem."
And in this way passed a pleasant day admiring each other,
The voice of the old world and the voice of the new.

"Shall we risk the parachute jump, Sholom?"
"Well, Markele, am I properly dressed for it?
Better we should go in the water a little maybe?"
So Sholom Aleichem took off shoes and socks (with holes—a shame),
Rolled up stiff-serge pants, showing his varicose veins;
And Mark Twain, his bathing suit moth-eaten and gaping
In important places, lit up a big cigar,
And put on a pair of waterwings like an angel.

The two great writers went down where the poor
Were playing at the water's edge
Like a sewer full of garbage, warm as piss.
Around them shapeless mothers and brutal fathers
Were giving yellow, brown, white, and black children
Lessons in life that the ignorant are specially qualified to give:
Slaps and scoldings, mixed with food and kisses.

Mark Twain, impetuous goy, dived right in,
And who could resist splashing a little the good-natured Jew?
Pretty soon they were both floundering in the sea
The serge suit ruined that a loving daughter darned and pressed,
The straw hat floating off on the proletarian waters.

They had both spent their lives trying to make the world a better place
And both had gently faced their failure.
If humor and love had failed, what next?
They were both drowning and enjoying it now,
Two old men of the two worlds, the old and the new,
Splashing about in the sea like crazy monks.

XVIII.

Marina Tsvetaeva (1801- 1941), "now regarded one of the best Russian poets of the twentieth century... whose Moscow childhood was punctuated by frequent and often violent family quarrels, and her poetic aspirations were belittled and discouraged... turned to Mark Twain's works—books bound in red cloth led to her escape into the world of her imagination. In 1908 she studied literature at the Sorbonne... and she wrote "Books Bound in Red" in 1909.

Books Bound in Red
Marina Tsvetaeva

From heaven of a childhood life
A farewell to me you're sending,
The ever-loyal dear friends
Within a red worn down binding.
On learning homework from school,
At once I ran to see you yet.
'It's late'—'Please, Mother, ten more lines'—
But happily she did forget.
The fires flicker in a lamp...
How nice it is to read at home!
To sounds of Greig, Schumann and Kui
I learned about the fate of Tom.

It's dark... the air is growing cold..
Tom's full of faith in Becky's joy.
Within the darkness of the cave
Wanders with torch Indian Joe . . .
A cemetery... owl is screaming...
(I'm scared) And now through hassocks flies
The punctilious widow's foster-child,
Like in a barrel Diogenes.
Lighter than Sun is the throne hall,
Over the graceful boy—a crown..
At once—a beggar! God! He said:
'Forgive, I'm heir to the throne.'
To darkness comes, who comes from her.
Sad is the destiny of Britain . . .
O, wherefore not amid red books
Not to go back to sleep again
Before a lamp? O golden times
Where sight is braver, heart is purer:
O golden times, I say again:
Huck Finn, Tom Sawyer, Prince and Beggar!

XIX.

To the reader:

Because I want to conclude this book with a deeply personal response to Joy Harjo's *American Sunrise* (spoiler alert), I pause for William Carlos Williams's *The Doctor Stories,* compiled by Robert Coles, a book I bought on a whim because the cover appealed to me. I could see myself as an intern, in white coat, holding a child. There is a story worth telling about the book and Dr. Williams himself. As told by Robert Coles:

Fifty-two years after the publication of *The Doctor Stories* (1932), Robert Coles enters the life story of Dr. Williams and writes an introduction:

"A great privilege (and actually turn of fate) befell me in the early 1950s when encouraged by a fine professor of mine—at Harvard—under whose supervision I'd written my undergraduate thesis to send a note to William Carlos Williams and ask him if he'd mind reading a college student's attempt to understand his poetry, especially the first book of *Paterson* (an epic poem too long to include in this book but well worth reading in conjunction with *The Doctor Stories*).... After a long delay I received a welcoming reply to come to Williams's home for lunch, received encouragement about my thesis and so impressed WCW that he encouraged me to go into medicine—a turn of fate indeed.

William Carlos Williams *The Doctor Stories*[16]
(another meeting with Dr. Williams)

Robert Coles, in his introduction, writes, "I'll never forget an exchange I had with Williams until my last year of medical school. He had been sick rather a lot by then, but his feisty spirit was still in evidence, as well as his canny ability to appraise a situation—anyone or anything—quickly and accurately...Then he regaled me with some (literally speaking "doctor stories", accounts of how they did their various jobs, the joys some of them constantly experienced, or alas, the serious troubles some of them had struggled to overcome; the satisfactions of x, y, z specialties, and conversely the limitations of those same specialties. I told my advisor at medical school about the meeting, and I can still those words, too: "You're lucky to know him."

RC: As were the working-class residents of Paterson. plain people who considered themselves lucky to hold a job, lucky to get by, barely...families who had one very important loyalty in common no matter their (ethnically diverse) backgrounds...an eagerness...a willingness, an eagerness to consider one Rutherford doctor their doctor, W.C. Williams, M.D. We who think of poets often look far and wide for their spiritual roots, their cultural moorings. Williams was one poet who made quite clear who his teachers were, where they lived, how they lived, how they affected him, helped him shape his particular sensibility: "Yet there is/no return: rolling up out of chaos,/ a nine months' wonder, the city/the man, an identity—it can't be/otherwise—an/ interpenetration, both ways."

---

[16] Williams, William Carlos, *Doctor Stories,* 1933, Introduction by Robert Coles, 1984, New Directions, New York.

Doc Williams becomes WCW the accomplished fabulist, anecdotist—and as well, the medical and social historian who takes the risks of autobiography. There were poems similarly harnessed, intended, and even a journal entry, as in this wonderful statement found in the *"little red notebook"* Williams the Rutherford school physician, kept in 1914.

"I bless the muscles
Of their legs, their
necks that are
limber, their hair
that is like new
grass, their eyes
that are not
always dancing
their postures
so naïve and
graceful, their
voices that are full of fright &
other passions
their transparent
shams & their
mimicry of adults
—the softness of
their bodies"

When invited to speak at conferences... he was shy, modest—afraid he had little to say directly to his colleagues, no matter how much he'd offered the world in general through his many and varied writings. But he was dead wrong; he had everything to say to us.

He opens up the world, our world, to us...—and so once again...say and say again: thank you Doctor Williams
  – Robert Coles, M.D. March 1984, Cambridge Massachusetts

To the reader:

Tears fill my eyes as I pause to write what Doc Williams has to say about poetry—this man who loves so deeply and understands so fully the most vulnerable among us, our children.

Williams writes about poetry as perceived by the doctor communicating with his patients (pages 124–126). A lengthy excerpt serves as the Introduction to this book (see page 3, but it is worth repeating here as an introduction to some of his poems).

The Birth
William Carlos Williams

A forty-year-old Para 10
Navarra
or Navatta she didn't know
uncomplaining
in the little room
where we had been working all night long
dozing off
by ten- or fifteen-minute intervals
her great pendulous belly
marked
by contraction rings
under the skin
No progress
It was restfully quiet

approaching dawn on Guinea Hill
in those days.
Wha's, Doc?
It do'n wanna come
That finally roused me.
I got me a strong sheet
wrapped it
tight

around her belly,
When the pains seized again
the direction
was changed
not
against her own backbone

but downward
toward the exit
It began to move—stupid
not to have thought of that earlier.
Finally
without a cry out of her
more a low animal moaning
the head emerged
up to the neck.
It took its own time
rotating
I thought of a good joke
about an infant
at that moment of its career
and smiled to myself quietly

behind my mask.
I am a feminist.
After a while
I was able
to extract the shoulders
one at a time.
a tight fit.
Madonna!
13 1/2 pounds!
Not a man among us
can have equaled
that.

Dead Baby
William Carlos Williams

Sweep the house
Under the rest of the curious
holiday seekers—
sweep under the table and the bed
the baby is dead—

The mother's eyes where she sits
by the window, uncounseled—
have purple bags under them
the father—
tall, well-spoken, pitiful
is the abler of these two

Sweep the house clean
Here is ne who has gone up
(though problematically)
to heaven blindly
by force of the facts—
a clean sweep
is one way of expressing it—

Hurry up! any minute
they will be bringing it
from the hospital—
a white model of our lives
a curiosity—
surrounded by fresh flowers

To Close
William Carlos Williams

Will you please rush down and see
Ma baby. You know the one I talked
To you about last night

What was that?

Is this the baby specialist?

Yes, but perhaps you mean my son,
Can't you wait until

I, I, I, don't think it's brEAthin.

I was so moved by these alive, plainspoken poems of Birth, Death, and the Terror of a mother that her baby isn't breathing, that I was moved to try my hand at a plainspoken poem of my own—the result, by an amateur (unedited):

A Poem After "Notes on the Refrigerator Door" by William Carlos Williams
Howard Schwartz

Why not give it a try I thought as I sat on the toilet to pee?
Yes, men sit on toilets, too.

It's more comfortable and you can read the paper or check your cell phone
in the middle of the night—it was 4:30.

On the screen appeared, as part of a book review by a
new author, a Canadian, writing notes to her dying mother
and I thought # me too, whole books so my family might know me better,
like Michel de Montaigne, my favorite philosopher.

Freud wrote there are no coincidences, but he also wrote he didn't understand
women at all, not even Princess Marie Bonaparte

a grateful patient, who helped him escape from the Nazis—with his books and

artifacts—to die in pain, but live a little longer in England on
Hampstead Heath,

which I visited with my wife years ago—a pilgrimage, an
Underground
(subway) journey and long walk up a hill to his home,

not a way station; as an atheist he didn't believe in an afterlife;
his legacy was Psychoanalysis—the importance of childhood
sexuality, dreams—

not as electrical gibberish, Harvard researchers' gibberish, but as the
Royal Road to the Unconscious—there are many roads;

but this is a poem not a lecture.
And as I sat to pee, I thought,

What a coincidence, I was just reading
WCW's poems in his book *The Doctor Stories,*

to include in my newest book
So not to waste the moment I sat to write at my computer

a note to include in my book
that will not appear on my refrigerator door.

In Memoriam: William Carlos Williams Note

"This Is Just to Say
I have eaten
the plums
that were in
the icebox
and which
you were
saving
for breakfast
Forgive me
they were delicious
so sweet
and so cold"

—William Carlos Williams

XX.
A Brief Introduction to *Paterson*

Although I've chosen not to include *Paterson*, a reference to William Carlos Williams's aim in writing his epic and one of his poems will serve as an introduction to his opus:

Epilogue

Those blessed structures, plot and rhyme—
why are they no help to me now
I want to make
something imagined, not recalled?
I hear the noise of my own voice:
The painter's vision is not a lens,
it trembles to caress the light.
But sometimes everything I write
with the threadbare art of my eye
seems a snapshot,
lurid, rapid, garish, grouped,
heightened from life,
yet paralyzed by fact.
All's misalliance.
Yet why not say what happened?
Pray for the grace of accuracy

Vermeer gave to the sun's illumination
stealing like the tide across a map
Note. We are poor passing facts,
warned by that to give
each figure in the photograph
his living name.

"Asphodel, That Greeny Flower"

William Carlos Williams' long, late poem "Asphodel, That Greeny Flower" is remarkable in several regards. It is the fullest example of his work in the variable foot and in the triadic (or three-foot, stepped-down) line, a breakthrough form he discovered in *Paterson, 2* ("The descent beckons...") and utilized for many of his poems from the 1950s. It is also one of the most beautiful affirmations of the power of love in—and against—the nuclear age, and one of the few memorable love poems in English written not for a mistress but for a wife: his spouse of 40 years, Florence Herman Williams, or Flossie.

First published in *Journey to Love* (1955), "Asphodel, That Greeny Flower" came into existence during a time of nearly overwhelming crisis in Williams' life. Originally, he thought of it as the fifth book of *Paterson*, gave it the working title "The River of Heaven," and planned for it to include "Everything left over that wasn't done or said—*at ease.*" He began the poem in March 1952, on a hotel menu in New York City, and worked on it for nearly two years. During those years his health, which had begun to break with his heart attack in 1948 and strokes in 1949 and 1951, continued to deteriorate. He suffered another major stroke in August 1952 and knew that he could expect further strokes—any one of them possibly fatal—at any time from then on. His mental condition was likewise precarious.

A bout with depression was exacerbated both by the recent stroke and by the injustices surrounding Williams' appointment as Poetry Consultant to the Library of Congress. The position was first offered, then withdrawn owing to allegations of Communist sympathizing, then offered again contingent upon further loyalty investigations, which were conducted but never evaluated, so that the year's term was up before Williams was able to serve. The situation tormented him with feelings of rage, powerlessness, and humiliation. On 21 February 1953, he was admitted to a private mental hospital in Queens, where he underwent psychiatric treatment until his release on 18 April.

Most painful of all, the old uneasy balance between confession and deceit in Williams' marriage to Flossie finally gave way. During his stay in the mental hospital, threatened by death and ready at last to let Flossie truly know him, he worked on poems, including "Asphodel," and wrote letters confessing past adulteries that finally compelled Flossie's full belief. The process must have been immeasurably painful for them both. Needing his wife to hold firm now more than ever, the poet must test her by buffeting and shaking her. "Having your love / I was rich," he tells her in "Asphodel." "Thinking to have lost it / I am tortured / and cannot rest." And so, in three "Books" and a "Coda," he writes to Flossie about the flower of the Elysian fields, the flower that grows also "in hell." The flower has a central meaning: "Of love, abiding love / it will be telling." In the first two Books he speaks of their marriage, their past, shared projects, triumphs, and griefs; in Book III he begs for forgiveness, but also writes movingly of desire, giving "the steps / if it may be / by which you shall mount, / again to think well / of me." The "Coda," then, is his gift to Flossie, made possible by her forgiveness of him. They approach the end, the "thunderstroke," together, and tenderly he seeks to reassure her:

Inseparable from the fire
　its light
　takes precedence over it.
Then follows
　what we have dreaded--
　but it can never
overcome what has gone before.

Reassuring her, he also reassures himself. Without Flossie's love, any attempt at final affirmation would be whistling in the dark; with it, although the dark remains real, the poet's voice rings with authority, soars in celebration, and nearly breaks in a quiet hymn of praise.

The threats of both physical death and the death of love are right at the center of "Asphodel"--and not just at the personal level, but also at the level of global destruction. The poem has a strong dimension of public, as well as private, utterance. Throughout, it confronts what Williams calls "the bomb," both the nuclear threat itself and all forms of "avarice / breeding hatred / through fear," all forms of cruelty, oppression, and repression. But against *thanatos*, the death instinct, again and again the poet sets eros; whether it take the form of art, medicine, discovery, or desire, eros is the force that drives the imagination, the force that counters death:

If a man die
　　it is because death
　　has first
possessed his imagination.
　　But if he refuse death--
　　no greater evil
can befall him
　　unless it be the death of love

>   meet him
> in full career.
>   Then indeed
>   for him
> the light has gone out.
> But love and the imagination
>   are of a piece,
>   swift as the light
> to avoid destruction.
>   So we come to watch time's flight
>   as we might watch
> summer lightning
>   or fireflies, secure,
>   by grace of the imagination,
> safe in its care.

"Asphodel, That Greeny Flower" is not, perhaps, a perfect poem. Some have felt its final vision of Flossie as bride, "a girl so pale / and ready to faint / that I pitied / and wanted to protect you," to be condescending. Furthermore, as a philosophy of life the "Coda" is problematic, for Williams cannot quite articulate what he means by "the light." But "Asphodel" is a great poem. It was written by a man in his 70s who had to type it with the fingers of one hand, who could sometimes barely see. Yet it is one of those extraordinary utterances that prove the truth of Keats' contention that the world is a "vale of Soul-making." As a young man, in *Spring and All*, Williams wrote, "Life is valuable--when completed by the imagination. And then only." Thirty years later, "Asphodel, That Greeny Flower" reveals a life completed by the imagination. Despite the ruin of the body, the made soul shines out indestructibly.

– Ann Fisher-Wirth

Wikipedia Biography

Williams was born in Rutherford, New Jersey to an English father and Puerto Rican mother of partial French descent. His work has a great affinity with painting, in which he had a lifelong interest.

He received his primary and secondary education in Rutherford until 1897, when he was sent for two years to a school near Geneva and to the Lycée Condorcet in Paris. He attended the Horace Mann School upon his return to New York City and, having passed a special examination, was admitted in 1902 to the medical school of the University of Pennsylvania, from which he graduated in 1906. Upon leaving Penn, Williams did internships at both French Hospital and Child's Hospital in New York before going to Leipzig for advanced study of pediatrics. He published his first book, *Poems*, in 1909.

Williams married Florence Herman (1891–1976) in 1912, after he returned from Germany. They moved into a house in Rutherford, New Jersey, which was their home for many years. Shortly afterward, his second book of poems, *The Tempers*, was published by a London press through the help of his friend Ezra Pound, whom he had met while studying at the University of Pennsylvania. Around 1914, Williams and his wife had their first son, William E. Williams, followed by their second son, Paul H. Williams, in 1917. Their first son would grow up to follow Williams in becoming a doctor.

Although his primary occupation was as a family doctor, Williams had a successful literary career as a poet. In addition to poetry (his main literary focus), he occasionally wrote short stories, plays, novels, essays, and translations. He practiced medicine by day and wrote at night. Early in his career, he briefly became involved in the Imagist movement through his friendships with Pound and H.D. (whom he had also befriended during his medical studies at Penn), but soon he began to develop opinions that differed from theirs and his style changed to express his commitment to a modernist expression of his immediate environment.

XXI.
Biography of William Carlos Williams (Wikipedia)

Interrupting my journey with William Carlos Williams at an arbitrary point frees my readers to continue the journey if they choose, and frees me up to take a new journey with a poet I have known since she was a young girl, Lauren Schwartz, the daughter of my close friend, her father, Robert Schwartz. She, a published poet, graciously responded to my request for some of her poems to include in this book and sent me the result of a workshop she took this past summer at the 92nd Street Lexington Avenue YMHA, with permission to use any that I liked.

What Do You Imagine When You Imagine
Your Life Without Me?

Poems
Lauren Schwartz

This book is dedicated to
my father

Forty-three poems that are a biography of Lauren's life of personal tragedies and victories, the death of her mother by cancer, her own cancer, the immigration of her grandparents, her early childhood in Brooklyn, a sexual molestation by a predator, her introduction to anti-Semitism, her mother the artist who painted their front door red at their home in suburban Teaneck, traveling abroad and dropping out of graduate school to cope with news of her mother Harriet's cancer, meeting a boy who stands her up, and meets a girl waiting for him at the same spot also being stood up by the same boy (a serial stander-upper, I thought)—they bond and the next she is gone, anticipating becoming an Orphan, A Simple Coda , after Sappho—Sappho wrote mainly love poems.... poems usually focus on the relationships among women, What Matters—dancing and grinding with a stranger, Joe—the voyeur; The Dalliance—another use of sex to escape pain, Stories We Tell—fiction as a pick-up technique; (with hidden truth in the stories) and then This is My Will, her boyfriend's telling her he was leaving her (the source of the title of her book), and her leaving him, traveling with her few possessions south and kayaking with strangers—a job she needs to support herself, journey to Miami Beach with her children and a new life—and the journeys that are this book.

Unable to choose—who could choose, or edit a life—I decided to reread forty-three poems (always a good idea, to reread) and treat them as the poet offered them to me: I choose them all and will make some personal reflections on the poems and relevance to my own life, so intertwined with the poet's and her family's life. Her book of poetry is now intertwined in mine.

1. "Allon Bakuth"

Before I knew
anything, there was this tree.

Before I was this body
this tree grew
inside me.

I sit cross-legged leaning
against nothing. Beneath this oak
all day I sit.

The Oak of Weeping grows
in Israel, where the healer, Deborah,
Rebecca's nurse's is buried–

I tell you
it grows deeply inside me.

In the morning as Harriet rests,
I ache for her
liver, her legs,
for her right arm reaching

for the left arm, she sacrificed,
My mother was optimistic
that one arm would suffice.

At night when she shrieks
between silences lengthen
I lie in a meadow of thorns imagining
her world hazy with doses of dilaudid.

Our hopes swirl in the sea,
dissolve, mixing
with the salt of us separately.

In my sleep, I hold her hands.
She wore the large jade ring,
her father gave her
on her right hand, and the gold wedding
band my father gave her on her left.

Now I take the band,
too loose on any finger, hold
her hand
as I polish five nails.

In her swampy room,
sweat mushrooms from her skin
Tight lines, drawn mouth, cancer's
mask etched on her face.

The silences
between sighs are brief—
we work, we eat, we wash
we try to love even death.

When I was small
she read Sonnets from the Portuguese
and Dylan Thomas
instead of fairytales at bedtime.

She named me Lauren
before I was born
unaware The Oak of Weeping
was rooted in me.

My wife and I visited Harriet shortly before she died and wept then as I weep now. I never read *Sonnets from the Portuguese*, so I Googled them and found Sonnet 43, which perfectly expresses Lauren's love for Harriet:

Sonnets from the Portuguese 43: "How do I love thee? Let me count the ways"
Elizabeth Barrett Browning

How do I love thee? Let me count the ways.
I love thee to the depth and breadth and height
My soul can reach, when feeling out of sight
For the ends of being and ideal grace.
I love thee to the level of every day's
Most quiet need, by sun and candle-light.
I love thee freely, as men strive for right;
I love thee purely, as they turn from praise.
I love thee with the passion put to use
In my old griefs, and with my childhood's faith.
I love thee with a love I seemed to lose
With my lost saints. I love thee with the breath,
Smiles, tears, of all my life; and, if God choose,
I shall but love thee better after death.

2. "I Come from Where"

My lips move,
murmuring lullabies, I hold

a newborn in each arm,
I too was once a polished pebble

In the womb, now rough
with rivulets of indeterminate

destinations, pockets of seeds
and dust. My eyes, sallow

and deep, flower from the bulb
of my heart. My arms

have been empty and full, where
I come from; it is typical to have

and lose in the same moment.
I come from where wraithlike ropes

restrained my arms. In silence
I hold everything.

I come from a boy who, in 1902, slid
from the ship's planks, moist with sea mist,

who later met a woman named Flora.
Study with intention, he

touched her face and folded her smile
into his breast pocket.

My face, I have been told
is her face—one face.

Flora presses her cheek flush
to mine, petal to bud.

Faint heart nere won fair maiden, perhaps love at first sight, two immigrants
searching for a home in each other's arms. Imagine having your lover always
with you—near your heart–and her face and smile folded into your
breast pocket.

How lovely is that line to hold unto forever.

3. "Still life"

My grandmother's Hadassah arms
held me so I could fly–they

became wings on which I could rely

Flora, what could possibly describe

her aroma? Powder, roses
savory and spice? Black tea and apricots?

Her hand
just beginning to wobble,

brushed tears from my face she
winced when that guy hurt me.

Her taste, a womanly mixture
of lipstick and coffee nip candy,

saved in her pocket from the mahjong
game or the Board meeting.

Her blue eyes bathed me,
her voice lulled me as she

told me stories of being a woman in law school and marriage.

She heard each word I said,
nodded with knowing. I wanted to

lick the spoon while she chopped
liver and lick the wooden bowl.

The bowl sits on my counter
holding ripening fruit.

I love this poem because it reminds me of my grandmother, her hands, kneading and rolling the dough for rugeleh and my mother, who played mahjong, let me lick icing on her Friday chocolate cake–after I scrubbed the kitchen floor. My grandmother didn't say much, but she listened and smelled good, and my mother, not

a professional woman, but a reader and fund raiser for the local
Cerebral Palsy organization into which I was recruited to babysit
for boys too old to be to be comfortable with a girl babysitter taking
them to the bathroom. I, just thirteen, helped a dysarthric boy, with
his Bar Mitzvah lessons and shared in his triumph as he mounted
the bema on his crutches to recite the blessings I helped teach him.
My mother loved opera and had scratchy LPs of Enrico Caruso
who she believed sang like her father—a Cantor I never knew. My
memories—evoked by Lauren's poems are the poetry hidden in the
manifest stories we keep as long as we love. Typing for me is a slow
process, but has the advantage of giving me time to remember—sort
of put them on the table to ripen, and become more delicious or
painful, as the case may be, over time, and to speak them out loud.

4. "Colorless"

I saw the boy from the Chinese laundry drop
his ice cream in the street, and I could tell it was a rare treat

because I saw him wipe the dirt with his sleeve and lick
the whole mess clean. I would never have done that.

My father was a medical student,
My ice cream sat firmly on its cone.

If I dropped it, he could get me another one. The difference
twanged in my small bod. I cried because it wasn't fair.

That instrument, the high pitch of injustice—I heard it
when the crippled Italian grocer was taunted by kids

unbound un their pleasure of watching her shake
her broom at them cursing and spitting.

The superintendent of our building scolded
all the boys and all who stood to watch.

My chest felt tender like on the first day of kindergarten
when the metal door slammed my pinky and broke it.

Ashamed I tried to hide and ran away from
Westminster Road and got lost.

I was five years old and on the streets of Brooklyn as dusk settled
on parked Chevys; a black superball bounced down a hill,

I followed untethered in a colorless wilderness. Irish mothers
in aprons noticed I was out of place and yelled

Go home...where is your mother?
Home was a circle collecting dust on a windowsill
of a blue room and I was missing
it. I wound back through unknown streets, watching pigeons peck
at pebbles in the deepening dark.

Five years old and Lauren can remember every detail of three traumatic events, the unfairness of being privileged; the pleasure the bullies felt attacking a crippled woman, and the mounting danger— she felt separated from her mother in the growing dark. It is a short story complete with unheard music to focus our attention of the danger away from the circle of light where she belonged like other children—with Harriet. (There is an uncanny sense that Lauren senses what is to come.).

5. "1966"

The room faces New York
Harbor, west from the top floor
Brooklyn brownstone. The flame
from Lady Liberty's torch flickers,
sparks seem to dapple the wall. papered
with clusters of lilacs and bluebells,
in a soft spinning light. lying
in bed admiring the Lady,
her green eyes shimmering
on the harbor, rippling,
lulling me
to sleep, the glow
of freedom
freckling my face.

The New Colossus
Emma Lazarus

Not like the brazen giant of Greek fame,
With conquering limbs astride from land to land;
Here at our sea-washed, sunset gates shall stand
A mighty woman with a torch, whose flame
Is the imprisoned lightning, and her name?
Mother of Exiles. From her beacon-hand

Glows world-wide welcome; her mild eyes command
The air-bridged harbor that twin cities frame.
"Keep, ancient lands, your storied pomp!" cries she
With silent lips. "Give me your tired, your poor,
Your huddled masses yearning to breathe free,
The wretched refuse of your teeming shore.
Send these, the homeless, tempest-tossed to me,
I lift my lamp beside the golden door!"

6. "Hide and Seek"

Ona rainy afternoon
they play in the lobby
of The Pavilion
on Upper East Side

The girl, the boy
the grandfather play their favorite game.

The girl, skinny legs,
mini skirt, cowboy boots,

gets lost–
no secret signals,
meeeooows

from the Grandfather,
no answers
no one to find her

lost on the wrong wing
of the building.

A man appears. smiles and offers
to help her find her way.
Come here; I'll bring you home
Elevator door shuts–
she notices
he punches the wrong floor.

Pushes hard
wet breath
hands bruise,
he unzips,
reaches up
skinny legs,

no echoes
no sound

Was this a repressed memory that became conscious as you sat to write these poems or, like Blasey-Ford, have you always known—and suffered the consequences, but not known how to express it.

7. "Nickname"

Mom, whatsa a Fuckingjewbastard? Harriet
moved away from the kitchen stove,
her dyed her falling in uneven p

from s bobby pins, beads of sweat on her lips.
Turns to face me in her shirtsleeves
yellow and green chiffon, her pregnant belly
in full view, she said, *It's not meant to be kind.*
My brother also called Fuckingjewbastard,
three and a half, "Mom, why do the kids

call us that name? Is it what people
in Georgia call New Yorkers?" Never *mind,*
My mother twenty-eight, swollen and harried

in migrainous dispute with LBJ, learned to cope
by swatting lies. We called my father Dad,
Others called him Doctor.

Vet Nam named him Major. School hurt me. The chair
I sat in hurt me. I daydreamed, wrote stories
for my brother, for me, and the only black boy I saw

in the lunchroom one day. Next day he was gone.
Returning from school on blowy afternoons,
trudging on the on the red dirt path, hot red clay

stuck to my tear- streaked cheeks. Bob Dylan
filled the house. I read poems printed
on album covers and watched vinyl disks spin, dizzy

with questions. Tucked behind the honeysuckle,
blanketed by the hum of, bees I hid. I toyed
with shades of green poking through

red patches of dirt and the wide ribbons
of marigolds, my mother had planted.
On a chilly spring day, my only friend

Janie told me as we skipped to school
passing the chain gang as they dug
the never-ending ditch.

My mom said I can't be your friend no more.
That afternoon the music changed,

I rocked myself, arms wrapped round
dirty knees, well hidden in my spot, in my yard,
Fuckingjewbastard, in the marigolds.

Once I asked my oldest grandson Alexander, the only Jew in his high school in Hattiesburg, Mississippi–three hundred miles from Pulaski Tennessee, the birthplace of the KKK—if he had ever experienced anti-Semitism. He said, "No, poppa Howie. My friends are not that way." But some boy painted that swastika in the bathroom, too cowardly to say Fuckingjewbastard to my grandson.

8. "Pieces"

Let it go—
how often have I heard
it no longer serves?
I can,
like the blanket I cherished
until my father said—*Big girls don't*

I wanted to please him.
I gave it up.

My mother set it aside in the bottom of a dresser drawer
slipped between her bras and panties,
keeping it, she said for the day I marry
I would marry. *Something old for under your gown*

We moved often;
the shrunken blanket with silk edges got lost.
The drawer and bras and panties are also gone.
My mother is dead.

Pieces float
in a private space
of light
or air.

Just like that, My mother is dead; but not lost in the private space of memory. We all hold on to Blankets or Batman capes, or Bunny rabbits—transitional objects, in rags and tatters that are the memories of our first object, our mother's smells and bodies. On death's door we dream of our mothers; corpsmen giving morphine to mortally wounded soldiers report that they ask for their mothers. We Are—big boys and girls and we don't wasn't to give up our mothers.

9. "The House with the Red Door"

Our house had aluminum siding
and black shutters. My father's patients
had a separate entrance hidden by a bamboo
fence. He was a child analyst with toys in his office.
My mother painted our front door red.

It was the last house on the block
before the underpass which divided
Black and White neighborhoods.
New Jersey's Route 4 shook
the house all day and night.

The house was a rendition of colonial,
columns with ridges collecting grit. A gold eagle
embellished the metal mailbox.
For years, I bowled with plastic pins
in an unfurnished living room.

The scent of my mother's beef bourguignon
wafted the red door after school,
the breadbasket was always refilled
on Thursdays with Malomars and Yodels.
Our house was crowded with neighborhood kids.

The Jamaican housekeeper's, chicken feet
stewing—the steam mingling with pollen in a ray
of sun glinting off the swing set out back;
Reggae music drifting as the kids played
baseball on the chalk lined yard.

In the basement turpentine fumes,
my mother's artist rags, intaglio
prints inked and printed on a Brandt press.
The patients playing
games with my father in the basement.

I thought I saw masked men
in our den after reading *In Cold Blood*,
well into the late hours. In the
morning the console TV was missing;
the red door was locked from the inside.

On Cold Blood was the day residue for the dream: but who broke into your house and stole the TV? Or—deeper, were the children your father played with the thieves who stole him from you? Dreaming is the guardian of sleep, so you slept through a break-in robbery. Did your dad or mom call the police to dust for fingerprints? About those intaglio, might these be the ones you saw?

10. "Rose"
Time wobbles like china teacups
in a cool breeze
blossoming
Painted rose—

petals of one
flower
folding in on itself
hiding the center
opening age.
Withered,
petals dangle and drop
quietly,
simply
leaving space
china white.

Rose is a flower and a name, my granddaughter's name, Sabine Rose, a poet too. Her youth is fragile, and I don't think I'll see her in old age, withered; but I fantasize she will quietly, simply fill the white space of her life with beauty and love.

11. "Why I Dropped Out of Grad School"

Simply put, to travel to ease the pain of witnessing the unthinkable but inevitable, her (Lauren's) mother's death; but she couldn't. (As it happens, I visited all the places Lauren did on a month-long vacation with my wife and three kids, enjoying my memories, realizing I was avoiding the poem of Lauren's feelings about her mother's mortality

and her own. While waiting six hours for a train she read from her
collections to pass the time...."

Pink and white pearl-pebbles pocketed
in the Atlas Mountains, a bright purple scarf
with bells, a bargain in Marrakech. Sand
from the beach in Essaouira which Nelson had pored
into a cloudy glass vial when he said goodbye
in Fez. Letters on onionskin air-mailed
to the American Express Office, blue and self-fold
aero papers perfumed with night jasmine I picked
from blooms from blooms over-hanging the writer's umbrella
table where we drank
mint tea, smoked hand-rolled cigarettes,
and forgot ourselves for a while. I wrote in my notebook;
I wrote letters and poems to my mother, to her illness
and thought about time with her. Time
with her so she could tell me more.
If there would be time for us, I wasn't sure.

12. "Shadow Orphan"

When the call came, I picked my brother up
from Newark Airport. My head exploding,
I imagined my mother's arm, dangling
like a rusty hinge on the right side
of her body.

Or the specter of Harriet
frantically brandishing her arm—

her head bobbing and nodding.
Her last arm a warrior's sword!

The red door, a portal to family, opens.
Her pocketbook is on the front hall table
and her glasses poke out, her fingers
printed on the lenses.

A painting of her hangs at the top of the stairs;
Harriet, at seven years old, her body
whole and intact. Two arms, two hands folded,
daylight stream through the blonde curls.

Shadow orphan
no one can hear
the explosions
in your head.

A strange reaction occurs to me: Achilles is enraged bereft and crazy with rage, when his best friend Patroclus—and perhaps lover—is killed in battle by Hector. The Trojans heard his rage, *exploding in his head* as he wielded his spears, killed Hector, and sacrificed his own troops in his blood lust. Harriet was a fighter, no longer a blonde child and better, I think, to remember her frantically brandishing her arm—her head bobbing and nodding. Her last arm a warrior's sword!

13 "Trade Winds"

High tide rolled
in the Ile de Mogador hushed Essaouira

in a dense miasma, I danced on scuds
of foam—tempting waves to touch my toes.

Following the gulls
on a trade wind, I climbed

the lookout. The muezzin
beckoned afternoon prayer.

I thought I heard my name
called but it wasn't me

who heard. Now, sometimes I will
hear my name and then return to

forgetting. I swore I would linger
on the lift of a gull's wing.

If not you, who heard the adult, was it you, the child, who heard her mother calling you in from play, not for afternoon prayer, but for a snack afterschool?

14. "Simple Coda"
After Sappho

I write to you of a white goat
as I wander these hills drawing you close to me
in this high desert.

In this high desert
I see you in fragments—
I collect ancient storms
and bone fill my pockets.

Sand and bone fill my pockets;
holes measure memory.
The day you never said goodbye,
leaving me wrapped in your simple coda.

Leaving me wrapped in your simple coda,
to wander this dry place,
these hills heard you
calla to me, pressing me flat to my breath.

A love poem to Harriet; what is the negative oedipal conflict but love of a girl for her mother? In Why I Dropped Out of Grad School Lauren wrote:

I wrote letters and poems to my mother, to her illness
and thought about time with her. Time
with her so she could tell me more.
If there would be time for us, I wasn't sure.

Yes, "holes in our hearts" measure the memory of those we've loved and lost.

15. "What Matters"

It was as if the hours
and days before the moment
the boyfriend arrived never happened, or
made no difference. I offered him water
to cool the heat, I felt rise from the collar
of his day-old shirt.

For instance, he didn't know about my fraught
week—my friend's double mastectomy.

He wanted to go salsa
dancing in the desert.
I thought of Miami nights—
urban Cuban movements,
women heavy-hipped
men grinding inside frayed trousers,
the slide of the trombone
and the conversation
I left at the door
the moment he arrived

Sure, let's dance
as if nothing matters.
Let's grind the flesh around
the frayed conversation
as if everything that matters
slipped out then door
the moment you arrived.

First, the words matter; cool heat, double mastectomy, grinding, slide of a trombone, dancing as if nothing matters—when everything Lauren cares about matters. Driving my four-year-old granddaughter to preschool, driving past a cemetery, she said, "Grandpa, hold your breath." "Why?" "Because there are dead people buried there." And I drove her to school to play with her friends.

16. "Joe"

You were tumbleweed\appearing out of nowhere.

Waiting in your Mercedes
beater by the dumpster,

looking in my window.
what did you see?

the stain of the Merlot on your lower lip
as I kissed you clean.

We know what Joe wanted, but what did Lauren want—a roll in the tumbleweed, or like salsa and grinding, relief (temporary) from thinking of *her mother's arm dangling like a rusty hinge on the right side of her body?*

17. "The Dalliance"

11 AM: Coffee and toast wait for you
I notice your shadow graze my studio window.

You tap the glass. In your inky hand
a rolled white paper.

The coffee is strong; the toast is seeded
and sweet. I'm glad you are here

but as always you make me uneasy.
What did you do this morning?

I did the laundry and wrote a poem.
The paper unfurls

as an offering—
New Mexico's dust and light.

You say we should
just go to bed

already. I'm glad you are here
but offering me your body

reminds me that your words
are what I love.

Why did I struggle to see who is who in this poem? Then; it is the poet the New Mexico artist with the inky hands who is willing to have—the dalliance (just go to bed with) with her because she needs it, but whose words he really loves. Is his name Joe, too?

    I diagrammed the dialogue as follows:

11 AM: coffee and toast wait for you.
I notice your shadow graze my studio window   Artist

You tap the window. In your lanky hand   Poet
a rolled white paper.

The coffee is strong the toast is seeded
and sweet, but as always you make me uneasy   Artist
What did you do this morning?

I did the laundry and wrote a poem
The paper unfurls as an—offering   Poet who accepts the offering–
New Mexico's dust and light.

You say we should just go to bed
already. I'm glad you are here
but offering me your body Artist speaking to the poet
reminds me that your
words are what I love.

The way I understand the last stanza, perhaps misunderstand it, the poet and artist are lovers—as in a French New Wave movie—over strong coffee sipped from a white crockery bowl, followed by a dalliance.

18. "Stories We Tell"

Once you came into focus
and I stared you deep—

I searched for a way to see past
the past you kept telling

me about. The bipolar/borderline
personality wife and the sick girlfriend
you said alienated you and kicked
you out on a brittle day in late September.

You mumbled something about a men's
shelter—a Jewish men's shelter.
But you often boasted in the beginning.
Whether to impress me or not

it just reminded me how sad
you are. Spending time with you was kind
of like paddling with only one
in the deep part of a lake.

Somehow, I knew not to take too much
stock in your memory or description,
after all, you said you wrote fiction.
I read the stories in the letterpress

edition you gave me on our third date.
The little boy you talked about moved me—
how his father was the hero who was always
missing. You told me it was all fiction.

What have we learned about the poet to help us understand this riddle, a puzzle with no straight edge to start with. Why does she need to work so hard to understand this sad man attracted to disturbed women who kick him out and then by implication cause his skid row descent into alcoholism?—is it even fair of me to use an analytic approach to understand this fabulist story; but a story that invites us *to search... for a way to see past the past you kept telling (rhetorical)?*

Lauren chooses to write the stanza in italics. Words matter: In stanza 4, "Colorless" the poet writes:

*I saw the boy from the Chinese laundry drop
his ice cream in the street, and I could tell it was a rare treat*

*because I saw him wipe the dirt with his sleeve and lick
the whole mess clean. I would never have done that.*

*My father was a medical student,
My ice cream sat firmly on its cone.*

Empathy for the boy and guilt for her privileged life

*Spending time with you was kind
of like paddling with only one
arm in the deep part of a lake.*

Empathy for Harriet who she longed for more time with

*The little boy you talked about moved me—
how his father was the hero who was always
missing. You told me it was all fiction.*

Empathy for the boy whose father always missing because she knew what it was like to have a father who was never missing.
   Lauren dedicated this book to her father.

19. "This is My Will"

I wasn't ready for this. I had been good. The legs of my chair sank deep into the floor. My cheeks burned.

The energy of the day became a fossil at my feet.

We ended up going to a bar. The woods were too private a place to part. We needed public knowledge of the event to execute the action in a perfunctory manner; a firestorm of emotion doused with strangers' eyes and ears. It was still light out. I had a long drive ahead of me. We ordered food. Perhaps we thought that eating would make up for what was lost or missing, or simply gone.

It was midafternoon, but the dim light in the bar swallowed the appeal of the steamy day playing in the woods. The mountains, the streams, the wet grass, and stone faded into the muted memory. Even under the icy mist of the waterfall. I was aware of the urgency between us. It hovered, always ready to dive and devour when I felt safe. It was the last day. I had maintained the silence I swore myself to.

We swam in the stream. We played hide and seek among the moss-covered rocks. We made love on the forest floor It smelled like earth;

it smelled like the sea. We were completely children. In the heat of the day, I knew he loved me.

We waited for the food. I smiled at the thought I had won this time. I had not spoken; I had not fallen into his security. I had been able to climb the slippery rocks without taking his hand. I knew he knew this. I knew he had seen me at last; and wanted me. I was conscious of my movements; I was aware of his eyes. I knew he was frightened because we had spent such calm, uninterrupted days and I had not spoken. I didn't bring up the unpleasantness. He looked consumed; his concentration pressed me like the weight of a book preserves a flower. I wanted to turn his gaze inward, away from my face. I was afraid my expression would reveal too much. I knew he was going to speak, and I was wary I would succumb to his voice that never failed to stroke the utterly human within me. He turned his fork upside down and right side up again and again, occasionally pausing to make a five-pronged indentation in his napkin. Patterns emerged. The volume from the jukebox increased. Three or four more people entered the room. The din of glass and ice punctuated our silence. He asked, *When you imagine your life without me, what is it you imagine?*

I should have left. I should have gotten up, pushed the chair in slowly beneath the table and said goodbye. I stared at his shredded napkin. The pattern was clear. We had done all this before. My eyes filled with then poetry of his voice, at his words. Outside of my body, I could see myself at his feet. I was losing. I didn't know the right answer. *I can't imagine anything,* I said. The walls of the bar spilled over the giant waves. *I can't imagine anything.* He stopped playing with his fork. *But you must. You have to.*

The waitress arrived with our food. He ate greedily. I sat transfixed in the yellow light. I said, *But I am supposed to win. I am stronger than you. I have the history of motion behand me. No,* he said, *this is my decision. This is my will.*

He pushed back his thinning hair with his hand. I thought, *he will be bald.* I took his napkin to dry my eyes. I twisted it into little balls. I built a pyramid on the salt sprinkled table. I wanted to leave. Instead, I stayed to argue, in opposite to my intention. I knew I was losing my resolve when he smiled and somehow, I wanted it all to happen, and for him to see it.

He paid the check. We left the bar. I tumbled into the air. I tried to breathe. I tried not to forget my original purpose, to be good. I ran. He followed me into the cemetery. I wanted to dig in the earth and lie down. He asked, *Do you hate me? I hate you now.* There was nothing he could do to calm me. He didn't want to; this was his victory. He said, *I'm going to leave you here.* I looked into his eyes. I could see no memory there. This soothed me and before he could I smiled. It was no more than a photograph; he turned away and began walking. There I stood, captured in a still.

This Will is meant to be a legacy to her lover, who had to be the victor. The leaving had to be his decision; but since she could see he already had forgotten—the love they had shared, and she believed (after Sappho) "Sand and bone fill my pockets; holes measure memory. The day you never said goodbye, leaving me wrapped in your simple coda." Her former lover's pockets bore neither bone nor stone; they were empty. She was stronger than him. The poet in the end thought of an answer to her lover's question *When you imagine your life without me, what is it you imagine?* She, the *remembered* (a

word used by Joy Harjo, the last poet to be discussed in his book)
with full pockets, will remember herself, smiling, watching—as in a
still photograph—walk away.

20. "Shuttle Person"

Summer fires have been contained
in the high desert. I'm on
the silt of the Big Eddy takeout along
the Rio Chama at 2 PM.
I am somehow with Sam, on a kayak
trip with some guy named Andy. Also
an older couple, perhaps in their late sixties,
but who can tell, another guy
Tom and his young son Evan.
A crew of folks who are going kayaking—
even though the smoke signals
danger, loss of property, and loss of life. Except for me;
I am the shuttle person.

I drive Sam and Andy to the put-in
and help them load their gear.
The river is low. No rain for one hundred
and sixty-four days. Andy lights a joint,
takes a hit, begins changing
into neoprene paddling shoes. Tom
and Evan arrive with the couple—
I'm listening to some bruhaha about the time
or if there will be time, and how many runs.
Sam squints, guesses four runs. Sam

dips one end of the paddle into the mud
and pushes off. I wave at his yellow sunglasses.

I drive forty-five minutes down river
to wait. I dip into the shallow Chama,
inhaling traces of woodsy smoke, and draw
peace signs in the mud.

Lauren is on the run after her break-up, with little or no money but feeling strong, invulnerable to the warning signals of a potentially lethal storm ahead—as, strangely, are the tour guides and tourists. The poem she writes is a nostalgic memory of a kayaking adventure while she works her way to New Mexico (I googled Rio Chamas tours). I was reminded of a rafting trip I took with my son and grandson, then eight-years-old, on the Yampas River, the last undammed river feeding the Colorado. We slept in tents, saw soaring bald eagles, and Alexander imagined animals in the clouds. And when a storm struck, we took shelter until it passed.

But Lauren drives down river and while waiting to shuttle the tourists back—remember the lethal storm is coming or is the storm a metaphor for another storm coming—she dips into the shallow Chama, inhaling traces of woodsy smoke, and draws peace signs in the mud.

Take-out at Big Eddy in Abiquiu, New Mexico

21. "Miami Beach"

I left town with the kids and the dog and the car.
The rest of it remained at the curb in piles—
my life dusting the lawn.

There was home, there never was.
The uncanny was our only destination

I had been blind to it, to what was not happening.
I was blinded by the way my husband shined
a false positive on every shit-show he entangled us in.
I planned to stay forever even if it killed me,
floating close to the wild jasmine

in the deep end of the pool. The sunbaked vapors
steeped my solitude in repeated scenes
of loss. home by home, what I saw was nothing—
and I changed my mind. Time
had made a tear in the sunlight.

We had to leave the future,
The one with no hope and all the houses
I imagined making my homes. We had to leave
without him. I bent the light
before the eclipse of nothing.

Jasmine calls me even as sunlight
wanes in the musty grammar of its scent.
Nothing interferes with a steadfast bloom
white petals protect me—
while I float

I've been intending to talk about Lauren's use of words, evocative of feelings; uncanny, shit-show, wild jasmine, floating, tears in sunlight, bending of light-an eclipse, and then the smell of jasmine—a steadfast bloom, white petals protect me—(not my shit-show husband) roses, petals, floating in a pool or in a kayak; words that she uses again and again in her poems; words that evoke body, its rhythms and smells—mothers and young children—Mother Earth; we are children at the end of life who long for our mothers. Doesn't floating begin in the womb? And what are the first parts of the body we grasp for life itself?

22. "Cancer"

The walls are chartreuse
    I picked the chip from my
Benny Moore catalogue
    the sheets on the bed match

the chenille blanket
    in my gentle green room.
Calms nausea. Green tea
    in a Russel Wright teapot

holds potent catachines.
    The sunlight filters
through slatted green bamboo
    as Florida pulses.

So sad, Lauren has cancer. She tells us of her surroundings, which she can control, and homeopathic treatment—green tea instead of chemotherapy. She is alone as her world, Florida, pulses, lives, on. Why is she alone?

23. "Slowly, as in Creeping"

I dream often of a window
with stripped blinds that fractured
the light curiously
across the century-old pine

planks in our bedroom. I miss you. The tension in sleep
is destined to vanish
with an awakened heart.

I dream often of blinds
and fractures, soft bullets
lithe and edgeless as lashed your eye.
A blue eye. I dream

Often of those eyes that, like the light
That blinds and fractures,
momentarily surrender
the native heart. Then, vanishes.

Did Harriet have blue eyes? Yes, she must have had blue eyes because the first sign of her cancer was a pathologic *fracture* of her arm—*the one that hung like a rusty hinge*, while traveling with Bob (I think it was in Israel, but does it really matter where?). I like Lauren not feeling she must tell her readers what I, as family friend know, but by allusion, *petals on the water and dreams,* mixed with plain-spoken, gritty prose—very much like psychoanalytic sessions where analyst and analysand together listen with a *third ear*.

24. "Morning after Chemo"

Bright hot lights peel the darkness beneath my eyelids. Morning too soon again. I stretch the long pull of muscle running down the length of my shoulder to my pinky finger. Sleep dissipates as the stretch yields to the body. *This is my body.* The all too familiar dread tiptoed on the glistening hardwood floor. Certain mornings were better than others. This morning is not. The four posters stood like sentries through the night; they did well. I notice as I inhale, *Still here.*

I pull the oat-pellet head pillow tighter to my diseased belly. The noise of the boys winds up spiral staircase and drifts under the crack in the door. I should be downstairs, making French toast and driving them to kindergarten. Instead, he is downstairs doing something because I can't. This is even more terrifying.

It takes time to adjust to the toxicity of chemo. Who is *he?* Her shit-faced husband she left because he wasn't there for her? His return more terrifying than cancer and chemo brain poisoning? Love is making French toast for your kids and driving them to school, and *he* is doing it, not her—shame and guilt as a result of the cancer too.

25. "Waking Up"

Icy bone
cold mornings
before you can
brush away bits of dreams

that had gotten mixed up in your eyes
and tangled in the night nest of your hair,
a small pounding thrums
in your middle-aged body
drum-rolls you awake.
The vibration strums you fear
into wakefulness
and the memory of fear
and the fear.

Perhaps she felt fear in her dream and awoke to the reality of fear
of—death. And a segue way into reliving her failed marriage.

26. "Marriage"

I.
You often brought me flowers
at week's end. Words were rare.

As the years rolled along, we jolted
on a pitted road. A field of featherless peacocks strutted ahead.

You emerged on a night of blackened waters
pooling, inky waves cresting, gray foam lapping.

had I dared to slip in again
seeping over and under and inward until I was filled

and waked, warmed and chilled;
you are here and not here.

II.

Your eyes bruised me blue,
you squeezed my throat.

I pressed my cheek on the cold marble
and studied your Cheshire-gloat.

Our children were hushed
while you hid your vodka in a coke.
You don't know what you're talking about—
you screamed as I dredged the moat you built to keep me out.

I packed the Kids and dog crammed
In and left.

III.

In your throat
there was a final breath, and as I

exhaled, a bouquet of wild red roses
bloomed between the spaces

in your heavy mouth. Thorns
razored your lips—blue.

You never imagined this fragrance
blown from my mouth, before you

picked and then morseled me
between your unwashed teeth.

Too sweet to swallow.
Too dense to digest.

27. "When the Sheriff Came to Throw Us on the Street"

My husband was sitting
at the kitchen table.
I say What are you doing?
Waiting
For what?
I don't know.

The Sheriff and the Sheriff's men entered
moved our lamps and pottery,
my children's toys,
my panties
to the front lawn.

He sat in a trance—
Immovable, finger locked
On a trigger.

The Sheriff's men
Locked the door.
Locked us out.
My wedding gown
sealed in a box for twenty years,

lay on the lawn melting
like wax in 100 degree heat.
What I finally did was leave.

To the reader:
I was a guest at Lauren's wedding. The rain stopped, the caterer lay a long white sheet on the still wet lawn; the chuppah was white; her simple elegant gown was white—the one thrown on the lawn by the Sheriff's men—Lauren was beautiful—we cried; But this courageous woman knew she had to leave with her two Kids and Maggie, her dog, on a:

28. "Journey to Perdernal"

Pinhole of light
offered by morning's
chronic a daydream;
I suddenly saw
He door was ajar.

I surveyed the heap
of ersatz homes
built on faulty thinking
ac collection of dread
strewn on unkempt...
I saw an oasis, New Mexico
desert home
glinting through
my camera's curtain.

The truth urged,
Leave it.
Volvo craned with twins, dog
and three cardboard boxes. He
helped pack

Talismans, Tibetan prayer beads, Tzit Tzit knotted
to remember
sparkled in in the rearview mirror.
Give me a good reason to look back...
Driving through Florida...Biloxi, Baton Rouge...we took our time...
just a white line
to where? I saw an oasis
New Mexico desert home
glinting through
my camera's curtain.

Why New Mexico? Is it because her brother, a surgeon lives in Santa Fe, or is it because:

29. "It Rains in the Desert"

Desert air makes for clarity.
I see the distance I traveled, and my despair

evaporates in the zeroes of no moisture. How will I
settle in this brittle air? Where am I

after drowning at sea level. I awaken
in the desert, my view is outlined by forests

burnt by wildfire which sprouts green
in spring. Before sunrise, I take Maggie

for a run to Bear Canyon.
It is so dry I see dragonflies crystallize

at dawn—I recall a lost chandelier prism
I found while unpacking. Maggie pulls me

back once again. *Let's go home;*
thunder wakes the world.

Monsoons bring white skies, kiss
earth's open, insistent mouth

with rain. I open my mouth to taste
and out comes Ahhhhhhw—

On the trail, the dog-walkers
hear me rolling through cacti

and thickets of sagebrush. Spring winds gently
push back clouds and mud dries to adobe,

laves and all. In the distillation of morning
the canyon sings.

Dawn lifts the draped night
revealing fresh costume. Coyotes howl.
Clarity and a fresh star—Ahhhhhh

and:

30. "Reclamation"

The White Place
Plaza Blanca...

Each step crumbles.
What is that hum?
A call

At this moment
In this place
Om, shalom, salaam.

Peace, safety, and wholesomeness are to be found in the dry desert if you open your mouth to receive the monsoon rains, listen to the canyons sing, and the coyotes howl.

31. "New Day"

The grey sky socked
us in for ten days
Me and the kids and Maggie.

Everyone said the stronger parent
gets he most hate
because they can take it.

Lauren's ex-boyfriend hated her, and her hateful husband divorced her, and cancer attacked her, because that's what cancer does—but Lauren, the stronger parent, can take it.

32. "Autumn's Letter"

October, the tomato blossoms
wither on their vines, Before
dawn the pear tree shivers
scattering a selection
of leaves.
Dew funnels
in tight pleats
of green grass.
I count caws
of creatures,
uncanny—
I blink
stars away—
doves coo
as I stretch
into the X
in my bed.

Not sure I get this one. X is the roman numeral ten; does that mean stretches to the max (back in algebra, if X is ten what is Y...) or that she is generation X?? But I like blinking the stars away—because when my retinologist is taking a picture of my optic nerve, she says, "blink, blink, hold still, and keep looking at the blue light." Google says: Generation X, or Gen X, refers to the generation of Americans born between the mid-1960s and the early-1980s. Gen Xers, which fall between Baby Boomers and Millennials, number around 50 million. Members of this group are approaching the middle of their working careers and potential peak-earning years. That fits Lauren, who has told us she is middle-aged, still autumn. But I like my free associations better than the facts, because I am eighty-two, well into winter, although I'm still capable of putting out a few blossoms and cooing a bit.

33. "The Wind Changes. The Clouds Deepen"

The sky is bluer than it was Tuesday. The clouds move steadily at a quicker pace as if to make room for the ample night. Here in my yard, my flower garden where once pink lips and lavender tongues bloomed, has deepened with hues of mackintosh and pumpkin. My pear tree, in a green umbrella, unfolds to reveal crimson accents. It dances with bluebirds and ravens as wind moves brisk air through drowsy leaves, ushering drowsy dust through my window and across my room.

lingering fingers
trace the curve of a heart
winter skies approach.

As winter approaches, *I daydream of spring.* Where I used to plant vegetables, flowers, both annual and perennial, rose bushes, raspberry runners and once watermelons, I've planted an orchard; a fig tree tall and elegant but no figs—not enough sunlight—so I cut it down and planted an apricot tree—no apricots, birds eat the young fruit before it ripens—so I planted peach and nectarine trees for the squirrels to eat—a riff on Bette Davis, Gardening *Ain't for Sissies*. I forced tulips, daffodils, and amaryllis bulbs in my greenhouse, yellow waterlilies in my fishpond, which my sixteen-year-old helper now tends.:

I've seen a few bluebirds bathing and drinking in a dish around this pond, but for me the start of spring is the cardinal.

"The Arrival of Spring"
Howard Schwartz

Winter is so cold
Ah, red cardinals appear
On my patio

34. "Winter"

High desert wind slaps
sun-charred cholla
bits of last night's snow
seep into the fissures
of my boots.

rail runners puff
dreams into lean hope....
I quicken my pace,
searching
for the scattered threads of home.
In the Sandias a watermelon moon sun sets.
A shawl of snow dusts
the ridge.

What can I say, I'm a Jersey guy? Winter sunsets are gorgeous driving south on the New Jersey turnpike because of the sulfurous pollution, but they are most gorgeous looking west from the Jersey side at the Palisades, sipping a cocktail or wine at an outdoor restaurant, with sailboats docked at its marina.

35. "On My Daughter's Birthday"

...reminds me of the birthday
you never had. Everyone forgets.
But I remember the cruelty of your birth,
the first and last breath.

Looking up at the Sandias
I see my will. I opened my eyes
when the blood from my womb
fell in droplets on the floor.

At twenty-six weeks
The inside me was no more.

A middle-aged woman arrived for her analytic session complaining of sadness and depression she couldn't explain. I knew her well and asked her if the time of year or month or date meant anything to her. After a pause, she said, "Yes. How could I not recognize why I feel this way? It's the date I had an abortion-we weren't ready to start a family-it was a girl-I always wonder what she would be like today twenty years later." She went on to bear two healthy children, but she never forgot the first she didn't bear.

36. "What We Found in the Old Brownie Camera 50 later"

How to pick from this collage of a life?

Image One: My father at age 18 with his hand on my mother's seventeen-year-old breast.

Image Two: Me at two standing on a chair in my grandmother's kitchen, leaning over the oil-cloth table, with my fingers in the chopped liver bowl.

Image Three: A view of Lake Mohegan and a rickety rowboat; my grandfather's bicep muscle melting in the emulsion.

Image Four: The ghosting of my mother's amputated left arm. An arm she needed for making intaglio etchings on the Brandt press in our basement.

(Which Bob bought her, and Harriet proudly showed me—two of those etchings hang over my older daughter's bed, now a guest room, to remind me of Harriet, the museum's we visited on Wednesday afternoons, and whose shows we attended. She offered to gift me those etchings, but I insisted on paying her for them in simple light wood frames.)

Image Five: Double exposure of me at Jones Beach wearing a frilly diaper cover, my father dipping my toes in the waves.

(# Me too at Jones Beach about the same age, but on a blanket)

Image Six: A shot of Whitey (Harriet's grandfather) on the corner of Mulberry and Elizabeth, in front of his store—"WASSERMAN Haberdashery" in handprinted letters.

Image Seven: Gert, who looked like Liz Taylor, with Whitey who looked like Burton, mamboing in the living room in New Hyde Park, Long Island.

Image Eight: Aunt Rhea, hair wound tight in a beehive, smoking a menthol, staring out her window in the Village: then one she would hurl herself from.

My life too; two suicides and bi-polar disorder.

37. "Child"

It is time.
I stir with the chirp
of restless birds. The light seeps under the door.
tip-toeing towards tomorrow
calling me to you

Is it time to feed the babies?
Is it time to move
your clothes packed in boxes, to the front lawn?

I listen
for your laughter
as the door opens.
There you stand
tall and lean,
with the surprise of morning
and what awaits you.
Still sleepy, I reach
for your small hand.
It is 4 AM.
You leave me, clutching the hand
of a soldier on his way.

38. "Boys"

Remove the dust
long settles on walls

windows, ceiling fans and
deep crevices of pottery.

Changing again,
I make space.

All the rooms are quiet
and clear waiting for them,

When they come home we will
be different—

We will lay down new dust
and rise

38. "Stars"

Skin stretches
tells the truth
of this life—
stitched across my
body

no longer
youthful and taught.
It is not ripe and round
like the rainy motherhood years

No, this belly tells
the tale of childbirth

(those that lived and died)
cancer; scars crawl around and around

Stars a billion eons old
each a point of light remains
sutured crooked
in this body.

39. "April"

Passover and Easter are gone,
Yet February
remains in my body. Chill
the color of steel, seizing warm
blood at slap—
the color of the Bronx today, bleak
I remember this color
from visits to my grandparents
home on Thanksgiving.
A long ride from the Brooklyn
in the maroon Chevy—
me glazed over in the back seat
staring out the window, seeing stories in the clouds.

A small child
on a cold day
stuffed into a peacock-blue
scratchy wool coat and leggings
with a bootstrap
and a chinstrap

of the matching hat
choking.

I learned of make the best
of things by telling stories
to the clouds.

40. "The Long Silence"

On April 25,1982, a man who said he was a poet
attempted to see a newly appointed Cardinal.
He wanted, he said, to show the Cardinal his poetry.
He was carrying a plastic bomb.

My mother never told me that I could continue to live
my life; she was so irate; she was so bitter.

She was very clear. She was furious that we would live
and she would die, unarmed, wrecked—wretched.

Why didn't I take her to the sea and let her drown?
Once she told me her fantasy of walking far into the waters

on the white sands of the Algarve.
I question why we did not stay there and let her die.

I knew she was dying, why did we not stay;
let her die in the soft sand or the blue water?

Instead we hired a van. Drove

the pitted road to Lisbon. Passing through a town called

Purgatorio, every rut in then road made her shriek.
I closed my eyes to hear. In the airport bathroom

I wiped her; On the plane, I held the spoon to her lips.
In the car to Sloan Kettering, she had no hands to hold.

The oncologist brought out the heavy artillery
the bomb he saved for last;
I still hear her shriek with my eyes open
or shut

after thirty years silence I still
want to know why

instead of walking into the sea
she chose the bomb.

To Lauren, dear Lauren, now that I've wiped my tears and can type a response; please forgive yourself, you did all a daughter could do; you the poet, or the oncologist did not throw a bomb; the cancer was the bomb. Your dad knew mom was dying and bought the time share on the Algarve that she never lived to see so she might live, however long, with hope. She was, as you write, "furious that she would die"; her fantasy of a peaceful death helped her cope with her rage against the inevitable death she could not fantasize away. You are your mother's daughter; your autobiographical poems—epic poems of resilience—are your mother's legacy, and I am proud that I can make it part of my book so you can join the pantheon of greats I've discovered since I exposed myself to poetry "which I didn't favor until I started to read it." If I were to write a dedication to What Do You Imagine... I would write:

"To the child who told stories to the clouds who became me the poet who told the story of her life (1959–2019) and still counting in Poetry."

XXII.
Poems by Peter Balakian and Howard Schwartz

After Zucchini
Peter Balakian
The New Yorker, March 2, 2020

My grandmother cored them
with a serrated knife

with her hands that had come
through the slaughter—

So many hours I stared at the blotch
marks on her knuckles,

her strong fingers around the
long green gourd—

In a glass bowl the stuffing was setting—
chopped lamb, tomato pulp, raw rice, lemon juice,

a sand brew of spices—
from the riverbank of her birth—

Can holding on to this image,
help me make sense of time?

the temporal waves
waves smashing and lipping

the pulverized stone; a bird dissolving
into a cloud bank in late day;

the happy and sad steps we walked

along the plaster walls and steel bridges,
the glass facades, highways of glistening money

the objects we caress in dreams
from which we wake to find the hallway dark,
the small light at the bottom of the stairs,
the kitchen waiting with a scent

of zucchini s sautéed in olive oil
onion and oregano,

a waft of last night's red wine—a gulp
of cold water to bring on the day.

A Poem by Howard L. Schwartz after Zucchini

Grandma's Hands and Rugelach
Howard Schwartz

Who is there now to remember my grandma,
Malvina Steckler, except my brother and me?

She died at age sixty-six but seemed far older
than me at eighty-two.

She suffered from diabetes and my mother
administered her daily injections of insulin—

irony or unconscious choice of career that I practiced
giving injections on an orange as a medical student when I already
knew how to do it.

Fear of death was a part of daily life in our two-family house in
Newark;
my mother lived in fear of her mother dying from another heart
attack—

her first was at age fifty-five and her last was
when the first aid squad carried her down the stairs

from the sunroom converted bedroom where she sat all
day looking out the window or sewing,

still able to see through her round steel rimmed glasses
secured by a silver chain around her neck.

I never saw her again and have no memory of her funeral,
but she was my protector, especially her hands,

nails clipped short, polish clear, unlike my mother's bright red
nails, fiery like her Hungarian temper.

Cooking or baking was out of the question; the exertion might kill her
but so, might depression, although no one thought that way then.

Hungarians are by nature stubborn people;
at least I have known only a few who were not.

The battles between my mother and grandmother were epic,
usually over whether she had cheated on her diabetic diet
or on overexerting herself baking while my mother was out.

We loved my grandma's rugelach,
a pastry made from cake dough, rolled and stuffed
with apricot or raspberry preserves and raisins, cut into bite-sized portions.

The procedure took all day, what with kneading rolling the dough,
spreading the filling and stuffing long tubes of it, baking and then slicing it.

I learned early that the best delicacies are labor intensive. I
don't remember proportions, but I do remember procedures
because I was her willing but guilt-ridden assistant.

I knew this was forbidden exertion for my grandma that would arouse my mother's wrath.

When discovered, a crime that could not be hidden—ah, that smell—my mother would furiously attack my grandma as suicidal

for attempting that energy sapping or maybe heart stopping project. It's funny that I can recall her attacking grandma, but not what choice words she had for me, her complicit assistant.

When she was angry with me, she would chase me wielding a wooden spoon,
but never catch me—protected by grandma's hands.

My mother knew the recipe and taught it to Dana, my oldest daughter, who several years ago gave me a tin of rugelach for Hanukkah with a note, Love from Grandma.

XXIII.
Poetry is everywhere

On Dec 19, 2019 Brian Lehrer on WNYC interviewed Joy Harjo, performer (saxophone) and writer, the first Native American U.S. Poet Laureate, member of the Muscogee (Creek) Nation:

A brief introduction, a poem and a portrait (Wikipedia)

"Consistently praised for the depth and thematic concerns in her writings, Harjo has emerged as a major figure in contemporary American poetry. While Harjo's work is often set in the Southwest, emphasizes the plight of the individual, and reflects Creek values, myths, and beliefs, her oeuvre has universal relevance.

Harjo's work draws from the river of Native tradition, but it also swims freely in the currents of Anglo-American verse—Feminist poetry of personal/political resistance, deep-image poetry of the unconscious, 'new-narrative' explorations of story and rhythm in prose-poem form." According to Field, "To read the poetry of Joy Harjo is to hear the voice of the earth, to see the landscape of time and timelessness, and, most important, to get a glimpse of people who struggle to understand, to know themselves, and to survive."

Few poets, living or dead, have blazed as many literary trails as Joy Harjo. A member of the Muscogee (Creek) Nation, she grew up in near poverty in Tulsa, Oklahoma, a background that deeply informs her work. In addition to numerous collections of poems, she has written an acclaimed memoir, a play, essay collections, and two children's books. She has edited several anthologies and has recorded several music albums. Inspired by poets ranging from Richard Hugo to Pablo Neruda to June Jordan, Harjo, in her generous work, remakes the world from a Native American perspective. Her passionate lyrics place her own struggles—especially as a woman and a mother—alongside those of her community, representing both with clarity, sympathy, and fire. Moving freely between the everyday and the eternal, her poems defy centuries of colonial deprivation, often excavating and incorporating Muscogee history, culture, and identity. Her surname, taken from her grandmother, means "so brave it's crazy." It is a fitting description for her body of work, which was recognized with the Ruth Lilly Poetry Prize in 2017. The following small sampling serves as a brief introduction to her wide range of poetry.

Photo taken on June 6, 2019, attribution Shawn Miller, Library of Congress

Ah, Ah
Joy Harjo

for Lurline McGregor

Ah, ah cries the crow arching toward the heavy sky over the marina.
Lands on the crown of the palm tree.

Ah, ah slaps the urgent cove of ocean swimming through the slips.
We carry canoes to the edge of the salt.

Ah, ah groans the crew with the weight, the winds cutting skin.
We claim our seats. Pelicans perch in the draft for fish.

Ah, ah beats our lungs and we are racing into the waves.
Though there are worlds below us and above us, we are straight ahead.

Ah, ah tattoos the engines of your plane against the sky—away from these waters.
Each paddle stroke follows the curve from reach to loss.

Ah, ah calls the sun from a fishing boat with a pale, yellow sail. We fly by
on our return, over the net of eternity thrown out for stars.

Ah, ah scrapes the hull of my soul. Ah, ah.

In her new collection, An American Sunrise (W. W. Norton & Company, 2019), Harjo writes about her poetry and career. I bought the book and read it in one night. The poem she read on the show was about her grandfather; another is an account of washing her mother's body, a dutiful loving ritual in the Creek culture, was particularly moving for me. Her comments about the character of a proper leader are political but the form and rhythm of the words are meant to move us to consider the interface of prose and poetry (about which I have commented elsewhere). There are many moving short poems followed at times by relevant historical/personal comments that I hope the readers will read if they are moved to buy this book. We are living in an era where many peoples (the Creeks believe we are all one people) are undergoing a voluntary Trail of Tears, refugees from Mexico and Central America, forced to leave their homes and start anew in a new place, only to be excluded by our xenophobic President.

Harjo begins her book with a poem:

Break My Heart
Joy Harjo

There are always flowers,
Love cries, or blood.

Someone is always leaving
By exile, death, or heartbreak.
The heart is a fist.
It pockets prayer or holds rage.

It's a timekeeper.
Music maker, or backstreet truth teller.

Baby, baby, baby

Before, though even words are a creature of habit.

You cannot force poetry
With a ruler or jail it at a desk.
Mystery is blind, but wills you
To untie the cloth, in eternity.

Police with their guns
Cannot enter here to remove us off our lands.

History will always find you, and wrap you
In its thousand arms.

Someone will lift from the earth
Without wings.

Another will fall from the sky
Through then knots of a tree

You will never sleep again
Though you will never stop dreaming.

The end can only follow the beginning
And it will zigzag through time, governments and lovers.
Be who you are, even if it kills you.

It will. Over and over again.
Even as you live

Break my heart, why don't you

President Trump admires Andrew Jackson for his military valor and has chosen his portrait to hang in the Oval Office, but he may be unaware that: As a General and as President, Jackson believed in the segregation of whites and Native Americans, according to NPR's Steve Inskeep, author of *Jacksonland: President Andrew Jackson, Cherokee Chief John Ross, and a Great American Land Grab*. He was ruthless,"opening Southern land for white real estate development, including his own personal real estate investments, whatever the human cost." His Indian Removal Act resulted in the "Trail of Tears," so called for the deadly journey that the Cherokee nation traveled after the law required them to give up their lands east of the Mississippi River and to relocate to what's now known as Oklahoma.

From *An American Sunrise:*

Washing My Mother's Body (pages 30–34)
Joy Harjo

(As this is a long poem, I will only transcribe parts of it, to get the feel of it and its importance to connect the dead with the living in the endless trail of history of the deceased through unrecorded time—through memory.)

I never got to wash my mother's body when she died
I return to take care of her in memory
That's how I make peace when things are left undone.
I go back and open the door.
I step in to make my ritual. To do what should have been done
what needs to be fixed so that my spirit can move on,
So that the children and grandchildren are not caught in a knot
Of regret they do not understand.

I find the white enamel pan she used for bread and biscuits.
It is the same pan she used to bathe is in when we were babies.
I turn then faucet on and hold my hand under the water
until it is warm. Then temperature one uses to bathe an infant.
I find a clean washcloth in a stack of washcloths.

Shen had nothing in her childhood.
She made sure she had plenty of everything
when she grew up and made her own life.
Her closets were full of pretty dresses,
So many she had no time to wear them all.
They were bought by the young girl who wore the same
flour sack dress
to school every day, the one she had to wash out every night
and hang up to dry near the stove.

I pick up then bar of soap from her sink,
the same soap she used yesterday morning to wash her face.
When she looked min the mirror, did she know it would be her
last sunrise?
I move her pill boxes, a clock radio on the table by her bed,
a pen and set down the pan. I straighten the blankets over her,
to keep her warm, for dignity.
I start with her face. Her face is unlined even two months before
her eightieth birthday. She was known for her beauty
and when younger passed form the Cherokee
that was through her mother and her mother's mother
all the way back to time's beginning.
My mother had the iron pot given to her by her Cherokee mother,
whose mother gave it to her, given to her by the US government
on the Trail of Tears.
She grew flowers in it.

I've been crying as I type, slowly hunting and pecking because I never learned to touch-type. It's not so bad because as I pause, I think of my mother, and the last time I saw her. She was eighty-four and had suffered from heart disease for ten years, disease that could not be cured by a stent, although her doctors tried. She suffered a post-op paranoid psychosis, hearing frightening voices through the hospital air vents, and tried to leave her bed. Her nurses said she'd soon calm down, but she didn't. I insisted she be given a sedative but couldn't write the orders myself. I couldn't help my mother who nursed me as a baby. She used her mother's iron pot to cook brisket until she was too weak to lift it. She was beautiful, a Hungarian girl who looked like a *Vogue* model when she married at twenty-three. Everyone who knew her thought she was beautiful. And she was courageous, a warrior fighting to live independently in her pre-war apartment on the upper East-Side. She was going blind from a benign optic chiasm tumor. She could no longer go to the opera she loved or the movies on 87th Street, but she insisted on going alone for difficult radiation treatments at Mt. Sinai Hospital by taxi. She needed a companion to stay with her at night to shop, clean, and bathe her. One of my close friends lived in a building directly across the street. My wife and I were meeting he and his wife for dinner, so I had time for a brief visit. Adele greeted me at the door, freshly bathed, smelling of the soap she used, Ivory, of course, her hair now white and combed strait down by her nurse. I kissed her good night. She died peacefully in her sleep that night, never to see another sunrise.

Harjo is lovingly intimate with her mother's body, the body from which she came.

I wash her feet, caress them
You will have some rest now, I tell my mother
even though as I know my mother was never one for resting. I cover her.

My mother was a walker too, her only form of exercise, until she couldn't. When she was discharged from Lenox Hill Hospital ten blocks south of her apartment after a brief stay for a coronary event, she insisted on walking, slowly, very slowly holding my arm. She held unto life as long as she could, and I admired her courage—but I offered more than once to hail a cab and held her more tightly at each curb as a proper son should.

Harjo:

I make the final wring of the washcloth and drape it over the pan.
I brush my mother's hair and kiss her forehead.
I ask the keepers of the journey to make sure her travel is safe
and sure.
I mask the angels, whom she loved and with whom she spoke
Frequently,
To take her home, but wait, not before I find her favorite perfume.
Then I sing her favorite song softly, just a few phrases,
one of those homemade heartbreak songs
where there's a moment of happiness
wound through—

and then I let her go....

My father was a dancer, a rhythm keeper. His ancestors were orators, painters, tribal chiefs, stomp dancers, preachers, and speakers. His mother was a saxophone player and painter in Indian Territory before Oklahoma statehood. All his relatively short life he looked for a vision or song to counter the heartbreak of history.

Rivers are the old roads, as are songs, to traverse memory.
I emerged from the story, dripping with the waters of memory.

I was moved by Harjo's "Rivers are the old roads, as are songs, to traverse memory" and recalled a journey I made on my 75th birthday, a journey to preserve the memory of strangers and my father, "The Man from Nowhere."

On my 75th birthday I walked through Green River Cemetery, in Springs, East Hampton, smoking a cigar, one of the few I treat myself to each year, and at a leisurely pace read the messages of the deceased to the living who might visit them. This small cemetery was established to inter the remains of the original English settlers who came in the late 1600s to this wooded peninsula near the Eastern tip of Long Island (South Fork). In this idyllic place, surrounded by harbors, bays, and the great Atlantic, they fished the sea and harvested the mud bottoms of its bays and harbors for clams, oysters, and scallops. Some farmed the fertile land gathering the indigenous potatoes to fortify their life sustaining and delicious chowders. These settlers called themselves Bonakers after Accabonic Harbor (a Montaukett/Algonquian Indian name used by the land's first owners), and this cemetery became their final resting place. Those Bonakers, named King, Lester, Bennett (and others) who came first as fishermen, bay-men, and farmers and remained to work as builders, tradesmen, plumbers, electricians, lawyers, teachers, potato farmers, and yet still fishermen, were gradually joined by others seeking a seaside or wooded retreat far-but not too far-from the hectic pace of their lives in the city (New York metropolitan area). Springs became the summer or all- year-round home for writers Kurt Vonnegut, Joseph Heller, Philip Roth, Nora Ephron, John Steinbeck, artists, (Jackson Pollock and his wife Lee Krasner,

Willem de Kooning and his wife Elaine, and others less well known to me), as well as executives, and lovers of sailing, reading, and fishing, professionals, socialites, and entertainers. The Bonakers provided the infrastructure and services they needed while they- the newcomers-provided the means to sustain Springs and the Town of East Hampton throughout the year. The final resting place of the original Bonakers, gradually became the burial ground of Gentile and Jew, the irreligious who did not feel the need for a personal God, the gay and straight who both suffered the scourge of AIDS, and the soldiers and sailors who also died serving their country in the scourge of wars. Although I did not feel it that day walking in the Springs Cemetery, I feel it as I write now that all cemeteries, as Lincoln in 1863 said at Gettysburg, are "hallowed ground" and that we should "honor their sacrifices [of those buried there] "so they shall not have died in vain."

I recognize that this introduction to a *Remembrance of my Father the Man from Nowhere* may seem tedious, as well as a romantic view of death and a nostalgic remembrance of the years I summered in Springs with my wife and our three children, surrounded by our friends, including the couple with whom we were staying that weekend. My mood that day (November 30) was reflective, not morbid or sad but perhaps resigned to my not imminent, but foreseeable death, limited by natural or accidental causes, but also hopeful that I would be remembered, not just by family or friends or some people I've helped, but even by the glance of a stranger like me who might read names, dates of birth and death, and pause to admire memorial stones in a place like this. (In this particular cemetery there were both formal and familiar granite tombstones and natural boulders set in carefully chosen settings reflecting the unspoken view that death was part of nature, no matter how it happened, and that life like the seasons repeats itself and goes on.) This rural cemetery will not be where my wife and I will be buried, but it is in a place that I know, can, and do often visit and always fondly remember. I will not be buried where my father is buried alongside my mother in another (once) rural cemetery where their parents and siblings are buried. I have often walked there, and my feet know the way to their graves, and there too I have read the names of strangers and thought what I thought that day I turned 75.

Harjo writes: My grandfather Monahwee (of some generations back) "visited his home in what is now known as Dadeville Alabama to stay there one night before being exiled to the West. He is reported to have said to a highly reputable gentleman, after gifting him with his portrait:

I am going away. I have brought you this picture—I want you to take it and hang it up in your house, that when your children look at it you can tell them what I have been...for when I cross the great river my desire is that I never again see the face of a white man."

After he left, he never turned back. He kept walking forward with his beloved people.

Joy Harjo knew who her grandfather—of some generations back—was, a man of principle and firm character who knew who he was and could write about the ideal qualifications for a tribal leader.

HOWARD L. SCHWARTZ, M.D.

For Those Who Would Govern
Joy Harjo

First question: Can you govern yourself?

Second question: What is the state of your own household?

Third question: Do you have a proven record of proven service and compassionate acts?

Fourth question: Do you know the history and laws of your principalities?

Fifth question: Do you follow sound principles? Look for fresh vision to lift all the inhabitants of the land, including animals, plants, elements, all who share the earth.

Sixth question: Are you owned by lawyers, bankers, insurance agents, lobbyists, or other politicians, anyone else who would profit by your decisions?

Seventh question: Do you have authority by the original keepers of the lands, those who obey natural laws and are in the service of the lands on which you stand?

XXIV.

Bless This Land
Joy Harjo

Bless this land from the top of its head to the bottom of its feet

From the artic old white head to the brown feet of tropical rain

Bless the eyes of this land, for they witness cruelty and kindness in this land

From sunrise light upright to falling on your knee night

Bless the ears of this land for they hear heartbreak and shouts of celebration in the land

Once we heard no gunshot on these lands; the trees and stones can be heard singing

Bless the mouth, lips and speech of this land, for the land is a speaker, a singer, a keeper of all that that happens here, on this land

Luminous forests, oceans, and rock cliffs sold for the trash glut of gold, uranium or oil bust rush yet there are more stories to be made little ones coming up over the horizon

Bless the arms and hands of this land, for they remake and restore beauty in the land

We were held in the circle of these lands by song, and reminded by the knowers that one is over the other, no human
above the bird, no bird above the insect, no wind above the grass`

Bless the heart pf this land on its knees planting food beneath the
eternal circle of breathing, swimming and walking this land

The heart is a poetry maker. There is one heart, said the poetry
maker, one body and all poems make one poem and we do not use
words to make war on this land

Bless the gut labyrinth of this land, for it is
                                  the center of unknowing in this land

Bless the femaleness and maleness of this land, for each the
fluent power of becoming in this land

When it was decided to be in this manner here in this place, this
land, all the birds made a birdsky racket from indigo sky holds

Bless the two legs and two feet of this land, for the sacred always
walks beside the profane in this land

These words walk with the backbone of this land messaging the
tissue
around the cord of life, which is the tree of life, upon which this
land stands.

Bless the destruction of this land, for new shoots will rise up
       from fire, floods, earthquakes and fierce winds to make new
       this land

We are land on the turtle's back—when the weight of greed
    overturns us, who will recall the upright song of this Lan

Bless the creation of new land, far out of chaos we will be compelled
to remember to bless this land

The smallest one remembered, the humblest one, the one whose
    voice you'd have to learn a thousand years by heart—we will
    begin there

Bless us these lands, said the rememberer. These lands aren't our
lands aren't your lands. We are this land.

And the blessing began a graceful moving through the grasses of
    time, from the beginning, to the circling around place of time,
al-
    ways moving, always

******

XXV.

Afterword
My favorite poems

When I thought of writing, as an Afterword, my reactions to certain poems, not already included in the main body of *Why Not Read Poetry,* I didn't appreciate how difficult a task I'd set for myself. How many poems? Living or dead poets? Modern era or antiquity? And whether or not I should exclude my granddaughter Sabine, an obvious favorite toward whom my natural bias would be to put her first on the list? I decided Sabine could hold her place with obviously more mature writers and leave it up to readers to judge for themselves. Then there is the technical problem of whether or not to copy and paste the poems or simply refer each poem by page number in the completed book, or am I procrastinating from the picking from my plethora of choices? The latter, I think. I started to read the poems, yet again, make spontaneous decisions, leaving the editing for last.

1) Sabine Bos: I still can't believe that a sweet, shy child could write:

Unreachable
Sabine Bos

I am strewn liked a blanket upon then universe
I dive headfirst into was and my fingers graze disaster
I compete with hope and I demolish sanity.
I thrive and flourish in the hearts of the weak

In the darkness I march triumphantly
My gun has unlimited ammunition
I am the immortal plant
A seed from within
Until I grow
I grow and I possess
I crank the gears of the mind
I tug and expose the impossible scenarios
Until imagination cracks from the pressure
I cannot be received for I am long gone
I am unreachable
I am fear

2) Sabine Bos, "Just Stand Up": I think of the teenagers protesting racial inequality and police brutality, lighting candles for those murdered in schools, synagogues and churches, seeking reproductive freedom, sexual choice (cis or other) as the bedrocks of democracy. Poets, writers, artists, and philosophers nurtured by teachers and colleges that value the humanities are not elitists; they are the necessary ingredients along with scientists and entrepreneurs that are the necessary ingredients for a civil society, a Republic which we must defend, or we'll lose it. (Benjamin Franklin). Hooray, Sabine.

Just Stand Up
Sabine Bos

What's there to see with your eyes opened but your mind closed off
You feel to touch but not to impose
What is a gift if you don't receive it

A candle is there but it isn't lit
Open your mind and don't close the door
You will be exposed to so much more
No steps back, keep running forwards
Knowledge is dangerous
A sharp precise sword
Don't open your mouth to say nothing at all
Respond to nobody's beck and call
You are yourself and no one else
A thick unique book on a shelf
Don't rip out the pages
Acknowledge the thought
It's a lesson that must be eternally taught
Questions directions they cut
Don't let them catch you
Just stand up

3) Abraham Lincoln-born 1809

Robert Pinsky, poet laureate (1887-2000) considered Lincoln, a poet since childhood, the "real thing." Lincoln, a depressive personality who suffered deep depressions during his adult life and, according to Jonathan Wolf Shenk, author of a Lincoln biography, "Lincoln went through three stages of depression. The first hit in 1835, when he was 26, and remained through the ups and downs of his early political career in Illinois. "I am now the most miserable man living.... I must die or be better," he wrote in 1841.

"The Suicide's Soliloquy

An unsigned poem, likely written by Abraham Lincoln , first published on August 25, 1838, in *The Sangamo Journal*, in Springfield, Illinois.

Shortly after Lincoln's assassination, one of Lincoln's personal friends, Joshua Speed, told William Herndon, Lincoln's biographer, that Lincoln had written and published "a few lines under the gloomy title of Suicide". No one had found the actual article. In 1997, independent writer Richard Lawrence Miller found "The Suicide's Soliloquy" and, in 2002, came to realize that it matched the descriptions of Lincoln›s missing article. Although it seems to follow the same themes and style as Lincoln›s other works, there is still controversy over whether it was actually written by Lincoln.

The following lines were said to have been found near the bones of a man supposed to have committed suicide, in a deep forest, on the flat branch of the Sangamon, some time ago.

> Here, where the lonely hooting owl
> Sends forth his midnight moans,
> Fierce wolves shall o'er my carcass growl,
> Or buzzards pick my bones.
>
> No fellow-man shall learn my fate,
> Or where my ashes lie;
> Unless by beasts drawn round their bait,
> Or by the ravens' cry.

Yes! I've resolved the deed to do,
And this the place to do it:
This heart I'll rush a dagger through,
Though I in hell should rue it!

Hell! What is hell to one like me
Who pleasures never knew;
By friends consigned to misery,
By hope deserted too?

To ease me of this power to think,
That through my bosom raves,
I'll headlong leap from hell's high brink,
And wallow in its waves.

Though devils yell, and burning chains
May waken long regret;
Their frightful screams, and piercing pains,
Will help me to forget.

Yes! I'm prepared, through endless night,
To take that fiery berth!
Think not with tales of hell to fright
Me, who am damn'd on earth!

Sweet steel! come forth from your sheath,
And glist'ning, speak your powers;
Rip up the organs of my breath,
And draw my blood in showers!

I strike! It quivers in that heart
Which drives me to this end;
I draw and kiss the bloody dart,
My last—my only friend.

I find Lincoln's history of depression, the reported timing of its onset, and Lincoln's reported suicidal thoughts convincing, albeit circumstantial, evidence, that he is the author of the discovered poem. I include this poem because of my professional experience and interest in working with patients several of whom have committed suicide despite intensive analytic therapy and medication. My speculation is that this poem was a sublimation of his morbid interest in dying in conflict with his determination to lead his country through a bloody civil war to preserve the life of the Union. What is his Gettysburg Address but one of the greatest prose poems ever written, to this day read out loud?

The Gettysburg Address
Abraham Lincoln

[1] Fourscore and seven years ago our fathers brought forth on this continent, a new nation, conceived in Liberty, and dedicated to the proposition that all men are created equal.

[2] Now we are engaged in a great civil war, testing whether that nation, or any nation so conceived and so dedicated, can long endure. We are met on a great battle-field of that war. We have come to dedicate a portion of that field, as a final resting place for those who here gave their lives that that nation might live. It is altogether fitting and proper that we should do this.

[3] But, in a larger sense, we can not dedicate-we can not consecrate-we can not hallow-this ground. The brave men, living and dead, who struggled here, have consecrated it, far above our poor power to add or detract. The world will little note, nor long remember what we say here, but it can never forget what they did here. It is for us the living, rather, to be dedicated here to the unfinished work which they who fought here have thus far so nobly advanced. It is rather for us to be here dedicated to the great task remaining before us-that from these honored dead we take increased devotion to that cause for which they gave the last full measure of devotion-that we here highly resolve that these dead shall not have died in vain-that this nation, under God, shall have a new birth of freedom-and that government of the people, by the people, for the people shall not perish from the earth.

4) The reunion of Ulysses and Penelope—*The Odyssey* – Homer

And as when the land appears welcome to men who are swimming, after Poseidon has smashed their strong-built ships on the open water, pounding it with the weight of wind and the heavy seas, and only a few escape the gray water landward by swimming with a thick scurf of salt coated upon them, and gladly they set foot upon the shore, escaping the evil; so welcome was her husband to her as she looked upon him, and she would not let him go from the embrace of her white arms. Now Dawn of the rosy fingers would have dawned on their weeping, had not the grey-eyed goddess Athena planned it otherwise. She held the long night back at the outward edge, she detained Dawn of the golden throne by the Ocean and would not let her harness her fast-footed horses who bring the daylight to people: Lampos and Phaeton, the Dawn's horses, who carry her.... Then resourceful Odysseus spoke to his wife, saying: 'Dear wife, we have not yet come to the limit of all our trials...

This poem is not only lovely but meaningful as an example of the consequence of PTSD before it was a diagnosis. Jonathan Shay, MD, PhD, a staff psychiatrist in the Department of Veteran's Affairs Outpatient Department in Boston. He learned from the veterans that his job was to listen as those who had similar experiences in Vietnam shared their suffering, and then informing the military and general public by writing two books about the ubiquity of the problem, *Odysseus in America* and *Achilles in Vietnam,* both of which I own. The military did not recognize this as an illness, like any other illness that needed treatment, usually group and individual therapy and medication, as would their families who have been affected by their instability, flashbacks and difficulty returning to civilian life and regular jobs. These insights are directly applicable to the PTSD of children subjected to sexual abuse and bitter divorces.

I did not become aware that I too suffered a mild case of Chronic PTSD until July 4^t, 2014 when I attended a concert at Lincoln Center of the US Marine Frum and Bugle Corps and the New York Philharmonic Orchestra. It was spectacular, the Marines in their scarlet uniforms and white gloves, shining brass instruments, marching on stage led by a trim Sergeant conductor. and I cried all the way through it. I said to my wife more than once, "They're so young. They could put down their instruments and pick up their rifles. They're marines." After the intermission, the conductor asked those in the audience who were in the military, or had a family member who was, to stand as the two orchestras played their anthems. I stood to sing "From the Halls of Montezuma...." My close friend Fred from Navy days at the Philadelphia Naval Hospital turned and whispered, "No. Anchors Aweigh" (The Marines do not have a medical corp. As a Lt. Commander assigned to head the admissions unit, my job was to evaluate marines fresh from combat with their glassy stares to long-term treatment or short-term treatment to prepare them to return to Vietnam where their platoons were fighting. They all wanted to go back. The unit housing my office was in a Quonset hut down the hall from a ramp attaching the huts to the main hospital where young paraplegics raced their wheelchairs. I signed the orders that might result in horrible death (Agent Orange), loss of limbs or worse, or chronic survivor guilt. I was identified with those marines and didn't realize it until that July 4th day. And to confirm my self-diagnosis, I was shocked to realize that in a long memoir I wrote I hadn't once written of my military service-my PTSD. So, I wrote a long essay: "From the Halls of Montezuma to the Shores of.... Vietnam": (*Hide and Seek/Hidden and Found-In Search of a Balanced Life-Psychoanalytic Memoirs, Stories and Essays*, IP Books, 2017, pages 87–103.)

5) Poems written by a former patient who asked to be identified by her name, Maureen Nelson, of her recovery from the sudden death of her husband of many years who fell off his bicycle on a humid summer day (from dehydration), fracturing ribs that punctured a lung, and did not survive surgery and led to Maureen's traumatic prolonged mourning. She would call me in the middle of the night to read me poems of her wish to claw through the dirt into his coffin to lie on her dead lover (they deserve to be kept private.) But after a year or so, she re-connected with a divorced man she knew before her marriage who was living in California and built a new life with him and his community of friends, an outdoor life of hiking and music. She taught me about Haiku and played games with me, back and forth-five-seven-five as she plays with her new partner.

Before and After
Sick to My Stomach
2013
Maureen Nelson

Just behind the screen is a woman in deep pain, if I let my guard down, she emerges fully depleted by the empty space her loss leaves her in. She pushes back, she pretends, she copes, but she is falling still into the abyss, into the space that exists between her and the man that once lived and will always be her husband, her soul mate, her essence, her reason to stay alive.

She knows that allowing the pain to swell does not, will not change reality.

I want him back, even with the challenges, the labor, the frayed edges; I want him back because what was good between us was so good, so vital, so special. Hours and hours, minutes, layers of years of sharing the stuff of life, this does not disappear because you are dead. The wonderful weight of the life we lived together tips the scale in our favor, why is no one listening.

Let me reach down into the earth and pull you to your senses. I want our life together; I want it back. I do not think I want to live without you, pushing myself forward into each new day without you makes me sick to my stomach.

Nothing, no one can fill this void, no one can stand in your shadow. Time does not heal, it only distances me from you.

Yet I can reach down into the earth and feel you right there,

Let me burro in.

Let me chew through the earth, through your coffin

Let me in.

PLEASE LET ME IN!

Or even better, COME OUT! COME OUT! WHEREVER YOU ARE!

I can manage, I can do, I can put up the screen,

but, don't know if I want to anymore,

If I let it, your death could eat me alive from the inside... the umbilical cord that connects us, you held fast in the grave and me stretching out towards a future...

Will I cut the cord, or allow it to stretch and strain between us, ripping at my insides until I explode and disintegrate eaten alive by torment and desperation.

Tomorrow is a new day. No, it is just another day to labor through.

More poems from Maureen Nelson, the writer of Haikus, who has fallen in love again and rediscovered her eroticism. She has offered a personal statement:

"When I returned to therapy after my husband died in 2012, I felt disembodied and I had lost touch with my libidinal self. With time, as I moved through my grief, I allowed that part of myself, along with my body as a whole, to return to life. Reconnecting with a long-lost love clearly awakened my sexuality and stimulated my desires and eroticism. This poem does speak to this awakening of desire; it is playful, lusty, and free, the way I feel when I make love to my partner."

Unnamed
Maureen Nelson
2014

Gather up my essence
Deep inside your blender
Lure me and stir me
Take me and shake me
Whip me and dip me
Blend me and bake me
Lick me and sip me
And then come back for more
To that place where I'll be waiting
Where time has no name
I'll be your protein milkshake
I'll be your healthy nosh
Like sweet and luscious candy
I'll be your honey baby
So drink me till you're full__

HOWARD L. SCHWARTZ, M.D.

The Man in the Moon
2015

Sometimes____
I feel illuminated
I could leap from crater
to crater
on the moon's surface____
Take rides through the
Night sky____
grab hold of the edge
of stars
and spin out of control__
This is how I feel
When you make love to me
Are you the man in the
Moon_____

6) Maxine Kumin—In the Absence of Bliss

In the Absence of Bliss
Maxine Kumin

Museum of the Diaspora, Tel Aviv

The roasting alive of rabbis
in the ardor of the Crusades
went unremarked in Europe from
the Holy Roman Empire to 1918,
open without prerequisite

when I was an undergraduate.

While reciting the Sh'ma in full
expectation that their souls
would waft up to the bosom
of the Almighty the rabbis burned,
pious past the humming extremes
of pain. And their loved ones with them.
Whole communities tortured and set aflame
in Christ's name
while chanting Hear, O Israel.

Why?
Why couldn't the rabbis recant,
kiss the Cross, pretend?
Is God so simple that He can't
sort out real from sham?
Did He want
these fanatic autos-da-fé, admire
the eyeballs popping,
the corpses shrinking in the fire?

We live in an orderly
universe of discoverable laws,
writes an intelligent alumna
in Harvard Magazine.
Bliss is belief,
agnostics always say
a little condescendingly
as befits mandarins who function
on a higher moral plane

Consider our contemporary
Muslim kamikazes
hurling their explosives-
packed trucks through barriers.
Isn't it all the same?
They too die cherishing the fond
certitude of a better life beyond.

We walk away from twenty-two
graphic centuries of kill-the-jew
and hail, of all things, a Mercedes
taxi. The driver is Yemeni,
loves rock music and hangs
each son's picture—three so far—
on tassels from his rearview mirror.

I do not tell him that in Yemen
Jewish men, like women, were forbidden
to ride their donkeys astride,
having just seen this humiliation
illustrated on the Museum screen.

When his parents came
to the Promised Land, they entered
the belly of an enormous
silver bird, not knowing whether
they would live or die.
No matter. As it was written,
the Messiah had drawn nigh.
I do not ask, who tied
the leaping ram inside the thicket?

Who polished, then blighted the apple?
Who loosed pigs in the Temple,
set tribe against tribe
and nailed man in His pocket?

But ask myself, what would
I die for and reciting what?
Not for Yahweh, Allah, Christ,
those patriarchal fists
in the face. But would
I die to save a child?
Rescue my lover? Would
I run into the fiery barn
to release animals,
singed and panicked, from their stalls?

Bliss is belief, but where's
the higher moral plane I roost on?
This narrow plank given to splinters.
No answers. Only questions.

Maxine Kumin (Wikipedia): An enduring presence in American poetry, Maxine Kumin's career spanned over half a century. Maxine Kumin (née Winokur) was born to a Reform Jewish family in Germantown, Pennsylvania. She attended Catholic and public schools before earning a BA and MA from Radcliffe College and married Victor Kumin in 1946 while still a student, and she would have two daughters and a son. On her early writing days, Kumin remarked, "began writing poetry in the Dark Ages of the '50s with very little sense of who I was—a wife, a daughter, a mother, a college instructor, a swimmer, a horse lover, a hermit."

I was born into an orthodox Jewish family. My mother's father was a cantor in Budapest and both of my parents immigrated to America well before the Holocaust. One day in 1947 when I was ten years-old my father introduced me to his second cousin, a muscular man built like a farmer or football fullback. My father said, "This is Hershey (the same name as mine, Howard, in Hebrew), He wants to tell you something." But Hershey was silent, so my father told me his cousin's story. "Hershey and his wife and young daughter were brought to Auschwitz, the extermination camp, and Birkenau, the slave labor work camp. Hershey was to be sent to the work camp, but before he was separated from his family a Gestapo officer shot his wife and daughter at point blank range as warning to this large man not to make trouble. Hershey did not make trouble, survived and married a woman. He told me they led a quiet life and did not have any children. I never saw Hershey again.

7) Robert Frost:

Robert Frost when asked what his favorite poem was, said:

Stopping by Woods on a Snowy Evening
Robert Frost

Whose woods these are I think I know.
His house is in the village though;
He will not see me stopping here
To watch his woods, fill up with snow.

My little horse must think it queer
To stop without a farmhouse near

Between the woods and frozen lake
The darkest evening of the year.

He gives his harness bells a shake
To ask if there is some mistake.
The only other sound's the sweep
Of easy wind and downy flake.

The woods are lovely, dark and deep,
But I have promises to keep,
And miles to go before I sleep,
And miles to go before I sleep.

Also:

Library of America Article in their Story of the Week
"Christmas Trees"

By Robert Frost (1874–1963)
From *Robert Frost: Collected Poems, Prose, & Plays*

In 1947 a student from the University of Maine, N. Arthur Bleau, attended a lecture Robert Frost gave at Bowdoin College. During the Q&A session Bleau asked Frost to name his favorite poem, and the poet declined to answer. But afterward Frost spoke to the young man privately and said, "I'd have to say, "Stopping by the Woods on a Snowy Evening" is that poem." Frost then related an anecdote, which Bleau records in an essay thirty years later.

In one of the early years of the century, three days before Christmas on the night of the equinox—in the poem, "The darkest evening of the year"—Frost hitched up his horse to the sleigh and, with a snowstorm on the horizon, journeyed two miles to Derry Village, New Hampshire, to sell some farm produce so he could buy Christmas presents for the children. Unable to sell anything, he returned home. "It had started to snow, and his heart grew heavier with each step of the horse.

Around the next bend in the road, near the woods, they would come into view of the house. He knew the family was anxiously awaiting him. How could he face them? What could he possibly say or do to spare them the disappointment he felt?

They entered the sweep of the bend. The horse slowed down and then stopped. It knew what he had to do. He had to cry, and he did. I recall the very words he spoke. "I just sat there and bawled like a baby"—until there were no more tears.

In a postscript to the essay, Frost's daughter Lesley confirmed the story, which her father had told her separately, also during the 1940s, almost "word for word" as it was told to Bleau.

My comment:

Why these poems? Because they so touch me; a loving father who weeps because he can't provide the Christmas presents his family expects. He weeps for them, bawls like a baby until there were no more tears, not of self- pity but out of empathy for their disappointment. His tears were the only gift he could give them, perhaps the most valuable gift of all.

8) **Life? or Theater?** by Charlotte Salomon, a monumental work of art, 800 gouaches, set to music, of a family's history of the Holocaust, a work of Modernism by 26-year-old Charlotte who was murdered at Auschwitz with her husband in 1943 which ends with a poetic

statement of empathy for her family and all the murdered Jews and others, "I Learned to Walk All Their Paths and Became All of Them."

Charlotte writing and painting Cotes D'Azur (age 26)
(April 16,1917 – October 10, 1943)
Murdered with her husband at Auschwitz

9) Warm Summer Sun by Mark Twain

Warm Summer Sun

Warm summer sun,
Shine kindly here,
Warm southern wind,
Blow softly here.
Green sod above,
Lie light, lie light.
Good night, dear heart,
Good night, good night.

Adapted from Robert Richardson's poem "Annette."

THE POEM ON SUSY CLEMENS' HEADSTONE

Photo from the Hurley Hagood collections

Mark Twain's daughter Olivia Susan Clemens died on August 18, 1896 at the age of twenty-four. She was buried in the Clemens family plot at Woodlawn Cemetery in Elmira, New York. A frequent question that arises is related to the poem that her father had placed upon her headstone.

The lines were adapted from a poem titled "Annette" written by writer Robert Richardson, sometimes identified as a native of Australia. The poem was published in a book titled Willow and Wattle, (1893). The original poem in its entirety reads:

Annette
Robert Richardson

AND they say, Annette, that you
Broke a foolish heart or two;
Can, I wonder, this be true?
Yet I will admit, Annette,
That you were a sad coquette;
Fain of praise and fain of kisses,
Fond of all the farthing blisses
That for fallen man unmeet are,
So they tell us, yet so sweet are
Fond of your glad world, and this is
All the blame I can recall
That on your young head should fall—
And I knew you best of all.
Save thought and little care
Than to braid your rippled hair,
Ribbon blue or crimson wear
Who in all this giddy fair
Who so bright and debonair?
Yet me thought, Annette, you were
just a little tired sometimes
Hearing of the midnight chimes
Weary of the passing show,
Tired of rout, and Park, and Row;
Longing for the night's retreat,—
Weary little heart and feet.
Dancing days are quickly run—
Dead, and only twenty-one!

HOWARD L. SCHWARTZ, M.D.

Ne'er so glad as when you had
Twenty lovers, man and lad,
Round you waiting for a glance
From your radiant beaux yeux
(Certes, they were very blue).
Twenty lovers in a row
Callow gallants, faded beaux,
I have seen them come and go,
Waiting patient for the chance
Of a single fleeting dance;
Mayfair's youth and chivalry
Bent to you their courtly knee.

Never more shall feet of yours
Lightly lead the laughing hours,
Lead the waltz's dreamy dance
To the " fair old tunes of France."
Dancing days are fleetly run—
Dead, and only twenty-one!

If that ancient ethic view
Of Pythagoras be true,
Your light soul is surely now
In that bird upon the bough,
Singing, with soft-swelling throat,
To the wind that heeds it not;
Or in that blue butterfly,
Flitting like a jewel by,
Flashing golden to the sun.
Soon, like yours, its day is run—
Dead, and only twenty-one!

Dead a week, and not already
Quite forgotten--nay, what right have
I to doubt it; sure, we might have
Easier missed a wiser lady.
Over you the grass will blow,
Springs will come, and autumns go.
Will you, Annette, ever know
There remain here one or two
Who will still remember you?—
O'er whose memory, now and then,
With a thought of sad, sweet pain,
There will cross your fair flower face,
And the bright coquettish grace,
With the memory of old days.

Somewhere there beyond the blue,
In the mansions that so many
Are, they say, is there not any
One of all, Annette, for you?
You, whose only trespass this is
That you loved the farthing blisses,
Broke a foolish heart in twain
That would lightly mend again.

Warm summer sunshine friendly here
Warm western wind, blow kindly here;
Green sod above, rest light, rest light,
Good-night, Annette!
Sweetheart, good-night!

Albert Bigelow Paine, in his biography of Mark Twain, notes that over the years the lines on Susy's headstone were generally attributed to Twain himself. When this was reported to him, he ordered the name of the poet Robert Richardson to be cut into the stone beneath them.

On January 22, 1907, when Twain was dictating portions of his autobiography, he recalled that he had forgotten the name of the author of the poem: "We had found them in a book in India but had lost the book and with it the author's name. But in time an application to the editor of 'Notes and Queries' furnished me the author's name... and it has been added to the verse upon the gravestone.

The last stanza of Richardson's poem is Susy's epitaph:

> Warm summer sunshine friendly here
> Warm western wind, blow kindly here;
> Green sod above, rest light, rest light,
> Good-night, Annette!
> Sweetheart, good-night.

Why this poem, another poem of love and loss by a humorist not thought of as a poet? We are living through a pandemic that has already caused hundreds of thousands of deaths around the world. Who doesn't know of a friend or child of a friend or a colleague who hasn't died, or hasn't read of couples who die within hours of each other? My wife and I are planning to make arrangements for burial, too long put off, so as not to burden our family–coffins, footstone or tombstone, messages carved in brass or granite. Most Jewish memorials are formulaic but creative license has its place. If my wife Susan predeceases me, Susy's epitaph brings tears and peace to me, "Goodnight Sue, Sweetheart, good night." I am not up to picking my own epitaph, but I have thought of a plaque on a bench in Maplewood's Memorial where these is a small Memorial to local residents who died in Vietnam. There are two benches where I rest before a final trudge uphill home. It would read, "Howard L. Schwartz, MD, LCDR, USNR, 1967-1969.

When my father suddenly died at age 66, he hadn't paid his dues to the Molly Schwartz Burial Society that owned a fenced-in plot in Mt. Hebron Cemetery in Queens, New York. He thought they would accept posthumous payment so he could join his family buried there. They wouldn't, perhaps a warning to other delinquent Schwartzes. You can't miss where his family is buried because of simple, elegant black marble slab, cruelly, jaggedly slashed three quarters down from its six-foot height as a memorial to his younger brother Samuel who died in the Spanish flu pandemic of 1917 and after whom my brother is named, Stephen Samuel Schwartz, Schmuel Avrum in HebrewebrewHebrewHebrew. My Aunt Rose, his older sister, and the matriarch of the family. made all the arrangements he hadn't and bought a plot near the Molly Schwartz plots for eight people, where only two people buried or ever will be. I have left directions ("My Feet Know the Way") and will set up a Perpetual Care Trust for my parents. My children or grandchildren have never visited Mt. Hebron, so there will be more stones on their graves—so sad, that only passers-by like me might read their names out loud and wonder why there are no stones upon their graves.

10. 10th and last poem—Jewish Humor—to be read Out Loud

Mark Twain and Sholom Aleichem
Edward Field

Mark Twain and Sholom Aleichem went one day to Coney Island—-
Mark wearing a prison-striped bathing costume and straw hat,
Sholom in greenish-black suit, starched collar, beard,
Steel-rimmed schoolmaster glasses, the whole works,
And an umbrella that he flourished like an actor,
Using it sometimes to hurry along the cows
As he described scenes of childhood in the village in Poland,
Or to spear a Jew on a sword like a cossack.

Sitting together on the sand among food wrappers and lost coins,
They went through that famous dialogue
Like the vaudeville routine After-you-Gaston:
"They tell me you are called the Yiddish Mark Twain."

"Nu? The way I heard it; you are the American Sholom Aleichem."
And in this way passed a pleasant day admiring each other,
The voice of the old world and the voice of the new.

"Shall we risk the parachute jump, Sholom?"
"Well, Markele, am I properly dressed for it?
Better we should go in the water a little maybe?"
So Sholom Aleichem took off shoes and socks (with holes—a shame),
Rolled up stiff-serge pants, showing his varicose veins;
And Mark Twain, his bathing suit moth-eaten and gaping
In important places, lit up a big cigar,
And put on a pair of waterwings like an angel.

The two great writers went down where the poor
Were playing at the water's edge
Like a sewer full of garbage, warm as piss.
Around them shapeless mothers and brutal fathers
Were giving yellow, brown, white, and black children
Lessons in life that the ignorant are specially qualified to give:
Slaps and scoldings, mixed with food and kisses.

Mark Twain, impetuous goy, dived right in,
And who could resist splashing a little the good-natured Jew?
Pretty soon they were both floundering in the sea
The serge suit ruined that a loving daughter darned and pressed,
The straw hat floating off on the proletarian waters.

They had both spent their lives trying to make the world a better place
And both had gently faced their failure.
If humor and love had failed, what next?
They were both drowning and enjoying it now,
Two old men of the two worlds, the old and the new,
Splashing about in the sea like crazy monks.

Dear Reader,

This Afterword might have been much longer, but I fear I have tried your patience too much already. At least I hope to have left you laughing.

www.ingramcontent.com/pod-product-compliance
Lightning Source LLC
Chambersburg PA
CBHW071958110526
44592CB00012B/1133